The Civil Society Guide to
REGIONAL ECONOMIC
COMMUNITIES
in Africa

Published by African Minds on behalf of
Open Society Foundations
224 West 57th Street
New York, NY 10019
www.opensocietyfoundations.org

African Minds
4 Eccleston Place, Somerset West, 7130, Cape Town, South Africa
info@africanminds.org.za
www.africanminds.org.za

ISBN:
978-1-920677-96-1 Print
978-1-928331-19-3 e-Book
978-1-928331-20-9 e-Pub

Copies of this book are available for free download at www.africanminds.org.za

ORDERS
To order printed copies from Africa, please contact:
African Minds
Email: info@africanminds.org.za
To order printed copies from outside Africa, please contact:
African Books Collective
PO Box 721, Oxford OX1 9EN, UK
Email: orders@africanbookscollective.com

Contents

Tables

Figures

Acknowledgements

The following current and former staff members of Open Society Foundations deserve special mention for reviewing chapters of the *Civil Society Guide to Regional Economic Communities*: Bronwen Manby, Pascal Kambale, Ozias Tungwarara, Mary Wandia, Ibrahima Kane, Nadia Nata, Josephine Ihuthia and Yaye Ndiaye. This guide was prepared from research by Morris Odhiambo (East African Community), Rudi Chitiga (Southern African Development Community) and Solomon Ebobrah (Economic Community of West African States). The final version of the *Civil Society Guide to Regional Economic Communities* was edited by Ali Zaidi and Marthina Mössmer.

Background

Revitalized regional integration offers the most credible strategy for tackling Africa's development challenges because of the many weaknesses that overwhelm the limited capacities and resources of individual countries. Collective efforts with dynamic political commitment to integration can help to overcome the daunting challenges.

– United Nations Economic Commission for Africa (2004), Assessing Regional Integration in Africa (ARIA I)

As regional integration gains momentum, there is growing interest among civil society and citizens to participate in the processes and programmes of regional economic communities (RECs). The constitutive treaties of RECs provide for citizens' participation, but the accessibility of REC treaties and protocols remains a challenge. Decision-making remains state-centric despite growing citizen and civil society interest in regional integration.

The *Civil Society Guide to Regional Economic Communities* aims to assist citizens and civil society in engaging with the policies and programmes of three RECs in Africa:

- The East African Community (EAC);
- The Economic Community of West African States (ECOWAS); and
- The Southern African Development Community (SADC).

The following are discussed for each REC:

- History and legal framework;
- Organs and institutions;
- The decision-making process;
- Budgeting and finances;
- Relationship with the African Union;
- Engagement with civil society; and
- Current debates within each REC.

The *Civil Society Guide to Regional Economic Communities* also contains a sampling of the experiences of non-governmental organisations that have interacted with these RECs.

1. Executive summary

Abbreviations and acronyms

AU	African Union
CET	Common External Tariff
COMESA	Common Market for Eastern and Southern Africa
CSOs	civil society organisations
EAC	East African Community
EACSOF	East African Civil Society Organisations Forum
ECOWAS	Economic Community of West African States
EPA	Economic Partnership Agreement
EU	European Union
NGOs	non-governmental organisations
RECs	Regional Economic Communities
SADC	Southern African Development Community
SADC-CNGOSADC	Council of Non-Governmental Organisations
WACSOF	West African Civil Society Forum

1.1 Regional Economic Communities

Regional Economic Communities (RECs) are the building blocks of the African Union (AU). The 1980 Lagos Plan of Action for the Development of Africa and the Abuja Treaty of 1991 establishing the African Economic Community provide the framework for Africa's overall economic integration.

The AU recognises the following RECs on the continent:

- Economic Community of Central African States;
- Economic Community of West African States;
- Common Market for Eastern and Southern Africa;
- Intergovernmental Authority for Development;
- Arab Maghreb Union;
- East African Community;
- Community of Sahel-Saharan States; and
- Southern African Development Community.

Given the relatively low level of literacy and exposure among their populations, the movement towards people-driven RECs is only achievable with the intervention and active participation of civil society organisations (CSOs) acting as a bridge between the RECs and the peoples of their regions.

These RECs have gradually evolved away from purely economic cooperation, which was grounded in their colonial past. Their evolution towards associations of peoples that aspire to true economic, social and political integration – people-driven RECs – has created a "virtuous feedback" that civil society can leverage to great effect. The level of civil society involvement in the RECs' agenda is still mostly in its infancy. This, arguably, is attributable to the fact that the processes and procedures of these regional blocs and the possible entry points for civil society intervention remain a mystery to many CSOs.

This publication aims to present an accessible, descriptive and analytic guide for civil society actors interested in the work of the following three RECs:

- East African Community (EAC);
- Economic Community of West African States (ECOWAS); and
- Southern African Development Community (SADC).

Each REC treatment comprises seven sections:

- Historical background and legal framework;
- Organs and institutions;
- Decision-making processes;
- Budgets and finances;
- Relationship with the AU;
- Civil society in the REC; and
- Current debates within the REC.

1.2 Historical background and legal framework

The **EAC** and **ECOWAS** have their roots in the economic and infrastructural links formed during the colonial period. Cooperation among the countries of East Africa dates back to the colonial period when the infrastructure for cooperation was put in place with the construction of the Uganda Railway (1897–1901). What is now **SADC** grew out of the struggle of the Frontline States to break the grip of apartheid-era South Africa on a de facto bloc of states under its economic dominance.

The three RECs are governed by constitutive treaties that spell out the objectives, scope, and institutional mechanisms for cooperation and integration, as well as fundamental principles and values. They also elaborate Protocols, Resolutions, Bills or Acts that are part and parcel of the treaties. The level of cooperation varies in the three RECs:

- The EAC Treaty provides for cooperation among the partner states in political, economic, social and cultural spheres.
- The ECOWAS Treaty provides for cooperation in political, judicial and legal affairs, regional security and immigration.
- The SADC Treaty aims at achieving common approaches and policies through protocols in areas of cooperation.

Having said that, in practice the three RECS appear to cooperate in the same areas; what is different is the depth of such cooperation.

The first legal regime for **ECOWAS** – adopted in 1993 – was replaced by the 2006 regime. However, the legacy of the first regime remains. On the one hand, under the 1993 revised Treaty regime, the highest forms of Community obligations were contained in the Treaty, the Protocols and the Conventions adopted by the Authority. On the other hand, forming the current regime are the instruments introduced by the 2006 reform of the Community's normative framework. Accordingly, Supplementary Acts are binding on Community institutions and member states while Regulations are binding and directly applicable in member states. This new regime is intended to transform the Community into a supranational organisation with organs or institutions authorised to exercise supranational powers in the sense of binding member states directly without the need for ratification.

The **SADC** Treaty was amended in 2001 to restructure its institutions and respond to new challenges such as poverty, gender, HIV/AIDS, globalisation, democracy and good governance.

The three RECS require existing and aspiring members to adhere to minimum standards of democracy, good governance, respect for human rights and gender parity. They also oblige member states to ensure other institutional reforms and capacity-building in key areas such as the judiciary, capital markets, deepening of financial inclusion, and peace and security mechanisms. Protocols and legislation at the regional level defining these standards are supposed to be "domesticated" through incorporation into national laws, regulations and statutes in the member states.

1.3 Organs and institutions

All three RECs have the following organs:

- A Summit of Heads of State and Government – the top political and decision-making organ – chaired on a rotational basis by the head of the "host" member state (supplemented in the case of SADC by the Troika, composed of the current and immediate past and future chairs);

- A Council of Ministers to advise the Summit;

- A Secretariat or Commission to administer integration and cooperation programmes and everyday running of the REC;

- A regional court;

- A parliamentary body – only the EAC Parliament enjoys legislative powers; the others are consultative or advisory.

ECOWAS and **SADC** have national focal points to enhance relations with member states and implementation of policies at national level.

Both the **EAC** and **ECOWAS** have established frameworks to facilitate civil society participation with criteria for granting observer status; observer status is, however, excluded in respect of the Summit of Heads of State and Government. SADC, on the other hand, is characterised by a state-centric approach in spite of Treaty provisions for people's participation.

1.4 Decision-making processes

An insight into the process of how decisions are arrived at in practice alongside a knowledge of decision-making structures is invaluable for CSOs wishing to influence and make an input into such decisions.

In the **EAC**, decisions are made by the key policy organs by consensus. The organs hold periodic meetings, which enable them to make decisions. Usually, decisions of a higher-level structure will be binding on lower-level entities. Decisions of the Summit, for instance, will be binding on the Council of Ministers. The Protocols of the EAC deal with specific areas of cooperation such as trade, land, setting up the Customs Union, Common Market, and so on. Different organisations have used different fora to engage with the EAC. Some have been granted observer status, while others have signed specific memoranda of understanding with the Secretariat. The *Consultative Dialogue*

Framework for Civil Society and Private Sector recognises the East African Civil Society Organisations Forum as the platform for civil society participation. Organisations have also taken part in drafting legislation and have been able to advocate for their passage through Private Members' Bills at the East African Legislative Assembly. CSOs with a legal and human rights mandate have successfully used the East African Court of Justice as an avenue for advocacy, particularly on extension of the jurisdiction of the Court to human rights. CSOs with particular expertise have joined working groups on some of the major issues of cooperation such as security.

In **ECOWAS**, the most important meetings – from a policy-shaping perspective – are the Summits of the ECOWAS Authority. The meetings of the Authority are normally preceded by meetings of the ECOWAS Council of Ministers. Council sessions have both opening and closing ceremonies at which public speeches are made. Though they may not make presentations themselves, this is still an avenue for CSOs who specialise in thematic areas to table pressing issues on the agenda of the Commission by lobbying the Council beforehand. The other influential institutions are the Council of Ministers and the President of the Commission, in that order. The bulk of decisions concerning the running of the Community emanate from the Council. The ECOWAS Commission, particularly the President's Office, initiates or at least has influence over all policy documents and legislative instruments that get to the Council and the Authority. The fact that all other institutions and non-statutory staff report directly or indirectly to the President of the Commission further amplifies the actual and perceived importance of this office. Although the ECOWAS Parliament is consultative, there are indications that it is growing in influence and will begin to play an important role in the affairs of ECOWAS. For instance, ECOWAS Parliamentarians are included in official ECOWAS election observation and monitoring missions.

In **SADC**, the Summit of Heads of State and Government is the supreme policy-making body. It approves policies before they are adopted into law. Civil society wishing to influence the Summit can do so through lobbying representatives of the member governments. Unlike the AU and other RECs, the agenda and papers for the SADC Summit are not made public. This makes it difficult to influence decisions of the institution. Often, influence at the level of the Summit is possible on political issues, but for other issues it is more effective to influence decision-making at lower levels. The fact that all decisions are taken at the Summit has caused some key stakeholders to express concern that issues get diluted as they go up the decision-making ladder. In addition, the perennial political problems faced in the region have resulted in SADC being seen as a political body in which economic issues have been sidelined. SADC decisions are made by consensus. However, there are some exceptions to the consensus rule. For example, three quarters of all members have to approve an amendment to the SADC Treaty for it to be passed. Decisions regarding admission of new members are based on unanimity. The SADC Treaty is silent on whether the binding decisions of the Summit have a direct effect on the laws of member states. In addition, SADC has no mechanisms to follow up implementation of the decisions of the Summit by member states, making implementation discretionary.

1.5 Budgets and financing

All three RECs are funded by a mix of contributions from international donors and member states. It is noteworthy that while the EAC and SADC are heavily dependent on donor financing (70% and 62% respectively), raising questions about their freedom from outside influence, ECOWAS is reportedly financing up to 87.5% of its activities through levies on member states.

EAC member states make equal contributions to the Community's budget. A new proposal to impose a 1% levy on imports of member states could, in theory, allow the EAC to become totally self-financing, but there are potential legal hurdles. The EAC pre-budget conferences, where budget priorities are determined, create an opportunity for civil society to take part in the process.

Since 2003, an **ECOWAS** Community Levy regime has been in place that requires member states to deduct and pay 0.5% of all import value from the national level to the ECOWAS Community Fund. ECOWAS estimates that its 2010 budget was largely financed by its own resources, as about

87.5% of the budget was financed with funds from the Community Levy, arrears of contributions and miscellaneous income, while only 12.5% of the budget was funded by development partners. The ECOWAS budgetary process is not generally open to external scrutiny and involves very little, if any, external participation, creating a perceived lack of transparency.

In **SADC**, the Secretariat prepares a Budget Outlook Paper every three years to ensure that there is balance between financial resources and the priorities set by both the Regional Indicative Strategic Development Plan and the Strategic Indicative Plan for the Organ. Drawing on the Budget Outlook Paper, the Secretariat prepares a corporate plan and a business plan on an annual basis. For 2011/2012, the SADC Council approved a budget of which 38% would be funded by member states' contributions and 62% by International Cooperating Partners.

1.6 Relationship with the AU and other RECs

The **EAC** has observer status with the AU. The EAC Secretary-General is invited to all AU Summits and is in charge of all relations with the AU. In 2012, the EAC posted a liaison person to the AU. The AU also has a liaison person at the EAC Secretariat.

The relationship between **ECOWAS** and the AU was formalised by the latter's 2008 Protocol on cooperation between the AU and RECs, and ECOWAS and the AU have agreed to cooperate and coordinate their policies and programmes. ECOWAS has specifically committed to deepening its ties with the AU; aligning its programmes, policies and strategies with those of the AU; and integrating with other RECs in accordance with the relevant provisions of AU Treaties. The ECOWAS office at the AU Commission is been operational since 2008 while the AU liaison office to ECOWAS in Abuja started its activities in 2014. The ECOWAS Mediation and Security Council collaborates closely with the AU's Peace and Security Council, and ECOWAS-supported military forces constitute the West African brigade of the AU's African Standby Force. ECOWAS and the AU have collaborated in military missions in Cote d'Ivoire and Mali.

The **SADC** Secretariat attends the regular Summits of the AU, including the January and July Executive Council and Assembly Meetings, as well as the annual meetings of the AU Commission, RECs and strategic partners. SADC and the AU have worked closely in areas of peace and security. For example, on the Zimbabwe crisis, the AU deferred to the SADC Organ on Politics to advise it on developments and recommended actions. The SADC Brigade of the Africa Standby Force was officially launched in August 2007. It was part of the AU deployments in Sudan.

1.7 Engagement with civil society

In their founding Treaties, all three RECs acknowledge the crucial role of civil society in helping achieve their economic, social and political integration objectives. They have committed themselves to involving civil society in decision-making and the integration process. More or less formal interfaces between the RECs and civil society have been set up in the form of the East African Civil Society Organisations Forum (EACSOF), the West African Civil Society Forum (WACSOF) and the SADC Council of Non-Governmental Organisations (SADC-CNGO).

The **EAC** has established a Department of Gender, Community Development and Civil Society to be the liaison with CSOs. The department works under the Directorate of Social Sectors. It also falls directly under the Deputy Secretary-General for Productive and Social Services, who in turn reports to the Secretary-General. As the focal point for civil society, the department has suffered from lack of capacity to handle the many requests for civil society participation in the EAC. The EAC Consultative Dialogue Framework for Civil Society and Private Sector provides for national and regional dialogues through the national ministries in charge of the EAC (national dialogue) and the EAC Secretariat (regional dialogue). The Framework recognises EACSOF as the platform for civil society participation and the East Africa Business Council for private sector organisations. At the end of each year, the Secretary-General's Forum for Civil Society and Private Sector brings together the different stakeholders to a meeting that makes resolutions on issues of importance to the stakeholders. These resolutions are then passed on to the Council of Ministers.

One of the main goals of **ECOWAS** Vision 2020 is to transform the organisation from an ECOWAS of states into an ECOWAS of people by 2020. This vision has brought about an increase in the actual room for participation of CSOs and non-governmental organisations (NGOs) in ECOWAS activities. Perhaps the most visible increase in actual participation is the growing involvement of WACSOF, as well as the increasing number of ECOWAS programmes aimed at creating greater awareness and involvement of civil society in Community affairs. CSOs can apply for observer status with ECOWAS. Such observers can influence decisions. They can be accredited to the ECOWAS Council of Ministers and may be invited by the Council to make an oral presentation. Through the President of the Commission, they circulate documentation to Council and may be invited to collaborate with committees. They may also, through the President of the Commission, submit questions or views for insertion in the provisional agenda of the Council and any other ECOWAS institutions, with the exception of the Authority. They also consult with the President of the ECOWAS Commission on matters of mutual concern. Despite the very elaborate provisions on obtaining observer status with ECOWAS, there are suggestions that in practice, organisations that have been engaging with ECOWAS do not necessarily have any official observer status with either the ECOWAS Commission or any other institution or agency of the Community. However, it would appear that CSO/NGO involvement is more in the area of implementation than in the area of formulation of policy.

The **SADC** Council of Ministers meeting in Luanda in 2011 declared that key stakeholders should participate in the SADC integration agenda through the SADC National Committees. This appears to block off direct participation at regional level, apart from existing arrangements with organisations such as memoranda of understanding (MoUs). However, CSOs can work directly at the technical level with departments. The SADC Secretariat has signed MoUs with some regional civil society networks, among them the SADC-CNGO, the Association of SADC Chambers of Commerce and Industry, the Southern Africa Trade Unions Council and the Forum for Former Heads of State and Government.

1.8 Current debates within the RECs

Integration in the **EAC** was envisaged through the Treaty to be a linear process involving three steps prior to the realisation of the Political Federation: the Customs Union, the Common Market and the Monetary Union. Many of the debates about the integration focus on subsequent processes, while some focus on the challenges that continue to face the process:

- *A two-speed integration process*: Kenya, Rwanda and Uganda have applied the principle of variable geometry on several occasions to make decisions that do not seem agreeable to the other two partner states, Tanzania and Burundi.

- *Multiple membership*: Three blocs with overlapping memberships – the Common Market for Eastern and Southern Africa (COMESA), the EAC and SADC – have commenced tripartite discussions to form one regional bloc that will encompass 28 countries with a population of 527 million and a GDP of USD 624 billion.

- *Consolidation or expansion of current membership*: The EAC restarted in 1999 with three member states, Kenya, Tanzania and Uganda. In 2007, Rwanda and Burundi joined to bring the total to five. Since then, Sudan, South Sudan and Somalia have applied to join the Community.

- *Rising poverty levels within a situation of deepening integration*: Trade between the partner states expanded from USD 2.2 billion in 2005 to USD 4.1 billion in 2010, but the distribution of the expanding wealth has not been equitable. If integration does not end in the advancement of the welfare of the people, then the EAC shall find itself confronting challenges of legitimacy.

- *Challenges in implementation of the Customs Union*: Implementation of the Customs Union started in 2005, but removal of non-tariff barriers continues to be a major issue of controversy.

- *Challenges in implementation of the Common Market*: The EAC entered the Common Market phase on 1 July 2010 after five years of implementation of the Customs Union. However, there remain disagreements over provisions involving free movement of labour. This is compounded by ongoing trade negotiations with China, the USA and the European Union (EU) that may undermine regional trade and increase poverty if citizens' interests are not secured.

- *Funding for the EAC and the issue of self-reliance*: The EAC's 2012/2013 budget factored in a member-state contribution of 29.06%. The contribution expected from donors amounted to 70.18%.

Current debates in **ECOWAS** revolve around:

- *Peace, security and stability*: Despite creating the Conflict Prevention/Resolution Management mechanism, the Conflict Prevention Framework and the Early Warning mechanism, ECOWAS has failed to prevent conflicts and crises in the region – as recent developments in Mali, Guinea Bissau, Guinea and Cote d'Ivoire have shown. In the absence of efficient preventive diplomacy or an effective West African Standby Force, ECOWAS's ability to manage and resolve conflicts in the region is greatly undermined.

- *Democracy and good governance*: Despite the democratic gains in the region, ECOWAS still needs to take concrete and effective measures to deepen democracy by reinforcing the rule of law, strengthening the capacity of regional human rights institutions and promoting participatory and internal democracy in member states.

- *Protocol on Free Movement, Residence and Establishment*: The realities faced by citizens when moving around the region sharply contrast with the promises contained in this Protocol. Challenges are inappropriate border checks, rampant corruption, violence and abuse of citizens by border officials and the expulsion of nationals from other member states.

- *Economic growth and the fight against corruption*: The Common External Tariff (CET) adopted by ECOWAS was set up to standardise taxation on all imported goods going into any member state, thereby protecting local producers and encouraging local consumption. With the high level of informal trade and the relatively small economies in the region, the CET should guarantee the effective protection of national economies from other regions such as the EU. The Economic Partnership Agreement (EPA) between the EU and ECOWAS signed in February 2014 may undermine efforts towards the CET and regional integration in the region.

- *Institutional framework*: The Community's current institutional framework is designed in such a way that the Commission largely dominates other institutions such as the Court of Justice and the ECOWAS Parliament. These institutions need to be strengthened.

Current debates in **SADC** revolve around:

- *Multiple memberships of RECs*: Most members of SADC are also members of other regional bodies, creating overlapping memberships that carry the risk of competing agendas. It is hoped the African Free Trade Zone Agreement (between SADC, the EAC and COMESA) will ease access to markets within the zone and end problems arising from the membership of multiple groups.

- *Negotiations with the EU on Economic Partnership Agreements*: Although SADC has 15 members, only seven are negotiating an EPA with the EU. The EPA negotiations are further complicated by the fact that South Africa already has a Trade, Development and Cooperation Agreement with the EU. This risks undermining regional integration aspects of trade.

- *The SADC Free Trade Area*: The Free Trade Area was launched in September 2008. Twelve out of the 15 member states are already participating; this eliminates tariffs and non-tariff barriers on substantially all trade, but progress has been slow.

2. The East African Community

Abbreviations and acronyms

AMISOM	African Union Mission to Somalia
APSA	African Peace and Security Architecture
AU	African Union
CASSOA	East African Community Civil Aviation Safety and Security Oversight Agency
CEN-SAD	Community of Sahel-Saharan States
CMP	Common Market Protocol
COMESA	Common Market for Eastern and Southern Africa
CSO	civil society organisation
EAC	East African Community
EACJ	East African Court of Justice
EACSO	East African Common Services Organisation
EACSOF	East African Civil Society Organisations Forum
EACT	East African Community Treaty
EADB	East African Development Bank
EAHC	East African High Commission
EALA	East African Legislative Assembly
EALS	East African Law Society
EANNASO	Eastern African National Networks on AIDS Services Organisations
EASSI	Eastern African Subregional Support Initiative for the Advancement of Women
ECCAS	Economic Community of Central African States
ECOWAS	Economic Community of West African States
EU	European Union
FTA	Free Trade Area
GDP	gross domestic product
IGAD	Intergovernmental Authority on Development
IUCEA	Inter-University Council for East Africa
LVBC	Lake Victoria Basin Commission
LVFO	Lake Victoria Fisheries Organisation
MoU	memorandum of understanding
NGO	non-governmental organisations
NTBs	non-tariff barriers
TIFA	Trade and Investment Framework Agreement

2.1 Historical background and legal framework

2.1.1 A brief history of the EAC

The East African Community Treaty (EACT) was signed on 30 November 1999, by then presidents Benjamin Mkapa of Tanzania, Daniel arap Moi of Kenya and Yoweri Kaguta Museveni of Uganda. It came into effect in 2000 upon ratification. The signing of the EACT was preceded by the establishment of the Permanent Tripartite Commission for East African Cooperation as per the Agreement Establishing the Permanent Tripartite Commission for East African Cooperation. The Tripartite Commission was responsible for the "coordination of economic, social, cultural, security and political issues" among the three founding states. It was this commission that evolved into the Secretariat of the East African Community (EAC).

Cooperation by the countries of East Africa did not, however, start in 1999. It dates back to the colonial period when the infrastructure for cooperation* was put in place. The preamble of the EACT partly captures this rich history. It shows that the integration of the EAC started with the construction of the Uganda Railway (1897–1901), the establishment of the Customs Collection Centre (1900) and the establishment of the East African Currency Board (1919), among other institutions. Indeed, the East African integration process was considered a model of integration, operating as it did the common services of over 30 institutions, including an array of research institutions.

Historians trace four phases of the initial integration effort, with the first phase running from 1903 to 1947. The beginning of this phase was marked by the completion of the Uganda Railway (renamed the Kenya and Uganda Railway in 1926). Various institutions were established before and after the commencement of this phase, all contributing to cementing relationships between the three countries of Kenya, Uganda and Tanganyika. These included the East African Posts and Telegraphs (1933), the East African Currency Board (1919), and the Customs Union (1917).

The period 1948–1961 saw a more structured cooperation and marked the second phase of integration. East African Railways and Harbours (created by the amalgamation of the Kenya and Uganda Railway with the Tanganyika Railway), the East African High Commission (EAHC) and the East African Central Legislative Assembly were among the bodies established during this phase. The second phase culminated with the three integrating countries becoming independent states.

History records that Mwalimu Julius Nyerere, the first president of independent Tanzania, proposed in 1960 (as Chief Minister of Tanganyika) that his country's independence be delayed to await Kenya and Uganda's independence to enable the three to form a federation immediately. This did not happen and the three countries attained independence separately: Tanganyika on 9 December 1961, Uganda on October 1962 and Kenya on 12 December 1963; Zanzibar attained its independence simultaneously with Kenya. Nevertheless, the East African leaders issued a formal declaration on 5 June 1963 to the effect that the federation would be established before the end of the following year, 1964. However, cracks in their united front began to appear when President Milton Obote of Uganda raised doubts about the project.

Phase three commenced with the establishment of the East African Common Services Organisation (EACSO) and lasted from 1961 to 1967. EACSO was formed from a restructured EAHC. During this time, most of the headquarters of the common services were centralised in Nairobi. The roots of disaffection deepened with the realisation that Kenya was benefiting more from this arrangement than the other two countries.

The structural challenges experienced at this point necessitated a rethinking of the cooperation, resulting in the signing of the first treaty and the establishment of the East African Community (EAC I) in 1967, initiating phase four of integration. Its collapse in 1977 marked the end of the fourth phase, followed by 22 years of separate development, until the signing of the EACT in 1999 between Kenya, Uganda and Tanzania marked the commencement of phase five of integration.

The following reasons have been given for the collapse of EAC I:

- Lack of strong political commitment;

- Use of different economic systems, which made it difficult to implement Community activities;

- Disproportionate sharing of benefits due to differences in levels of development and lack of resources to address this imbalance;

- Lack of strong participation by the private sector and civil society; and

- Ideological differences (Cold War politics pitting so-called East versus West with Kenya learning towards Western capitalism, Tanzania practising socialism, and Uganda somewhere in between).

The revival of the EAC (phase five) via the signing of the EACT in 1999 has its roots in the 1984 Mediation Agreement, which enabled the sharing of assets and liabilities of the defunct EAC I. The agreement anticipated future cooperation and enabled consultation between the heads of state of the three countries in Harare, Zimbabwe, during a meeting of Commonwealth Heads of State in 1991. The heads of state agreed on the revival of cooperation. A follow-up meeting took place in Nairobi in November 1991. This meeting issued a formal communiqué to revive cooperation and set up a committee to iron out the details. On 30 November 1993, the Agreement for East African Cooperation was signed. The Permanent Tripartite Commission for East African Cooperation was set up in Arusha. The Commission evolved into the Secretariat of the EAC.

The signing of the EACT gave impetus to the integration process. Subsequently, the Customs Union was established in January 2005 (the Protocol on the Establishment of the Customs Union was signed on 2 March 2004 and came into effect on 1 January 2005), while the Common Market was established in 2010. The next step of integration – the East African Monetary Union – was scheduled to come into effect towards the end of 2012 but was delayed. The Political Federation is anticipated to be in place thereafter. Table 2.1 summarises the phases, dates and establishment of institutions of the EAC over time.

Table 2.1 Different phases in the formation of the EAC

Phase	Some of the entities established	Year
Phase I: 1903–1947	Customs Collection Centre	1900
	Customs Union	1917
	East African Currency Board	1919
	Governors Conference	1926
	East African Posts and Telegraphs	1933
	East African Airways	1946
Phase II: 1948–1961	East African High Commission	1948
	East African Central Legislative Assembly	1948
Phase III: 1961–1967	East African Common Services Organisation	1961
Phase IV: 1967–1977	EAC I Treaty signed	1967
	EAC I disintegrates	1977
	East African Community Mediation Agreement	1984
	Permanent Tripartite Commission for East African Cooperation	1993
Phase V: 1999–	EAC II Treaty signed	1999
	EAC II Treaty enters into force	2000
	Customs Union protocol signed	2004
	Customs Union comes into effect	2005
	Rwanda and Burundi become members	2007
	Common Market protocol signed	2009
	Common Market comes into effect	2010
	Monetary Union protocol signed	2013

Rwanda and Burundi joined the Community in 2007. Before joining the EAC, Rwanda had applied to join the Southern African Development Community (SADC) but withdrew its application. For these two countries, the following factors propelled them to join the Community:

- Proximity to the three initial members (Rwanda shares a boundary with Uganda, Burundi with Tanzania);

- Shared resources (Burundi shares Lake Tanganyika with Tanzania);

- Being landlocked and therefore depending on the infrastructure of other partner states (especially the port facilities in Mombasa and Dar es Salaam);

- Opportunities for economic advancement; and

- Shared languages (Kiswahili, the national language in Kenya and Tanzania, is also spoken in Burundi and Rwanda) and therefore cultural exchange.

To some extent, the need to deal conclusively with armed conflicts in Burundi was also a consideration. Sudan, South Sudan (after its independence from Sudan), Ethiopia and Somalia have also applied to join the Community. This demonstrates its potential for further expansion.

2.1.2 Legal framework of the EAC

The EACT is the key legal document of the EAC. The Preamble gives the background to the EAC, elaborates the reasons why the initial EAC I collapsed and underscores the need to revive the Community. Interestingly, the Preamble states lack of participation of civil society and the private sector as among the reasons for the collapse of EAC I.

Briefly, the architecture of the EACT presents a logical flow such that the first articles establish the Community and give it recognition (Article 2(1)) and legal authority (Article 4(1–3)). Detailing the objectives and the principles (Articles 6 and 7) of the Community further gives it conceptual grounding, purpose and direction. The fundamental principles are laid down with a clear focus on avoiding some of the challenges that befell EAC I. Emphasis on mutual respect, political will and sovereign equality is combined with expectations of equal distribution of benefits and the need to cooperate fully for mutual benefit.

The vision of the EACT is that of a prosperous, competitive, secure and politically united East Africa focusing its efforts on improving the quality of life of its citizens through increased competitiveness, value-added production, trade and investment. The Community operates under the following fundamental principles:

- Mutual trust, political will and sovereign equality;

- Peaceful coexistence and good neighbourliness;

- Peaceful settlement of disputes;

- Good governance, including adherence to the principles of democracy, the rule of law, accountability, transparency, social justice, equal opportunities, gender equality, as well as the recognition, promotion and protection of human and people's rights in accordance with the provisions of the African Charter on Human and Peoples' Rights;

- Equal distribution of benefits; and

- Cooperation for mutual benefit.

The emphasis on good governance, rule of law, accountability and social justice is of particular interest to civil society. This framework provides a basis to hold the EAC partner states to account to citizens.

The Community is also grounded on the following operational principles:

- People-centred and market-driven cooperation;
- The provision by the partner states of an adequate and appropriate enabling environment, such as conducive policies and basic infrastructure;
- The establishment of an export-orientated economy for the partner states in which there is free movement of goods, persons, labour, services, capital, information and technology;
- The principle of subsidiarity with emphasis on multi-level participation and the involvement of a wide range of stakeholders in the process of integration;
- The principle of variable geometry, which allows for progression in cooperation among groups within the Community for wider integration in various fields and at different speeds;
- The equitable distribution of benefits accruing or to be derived from the operations of the Community and measures to address economic imbalances that may arise from such operations;
- The principle of complementarity; and
- The principle of asymmetry.

Essentially, these principles are aimed at guiding the operations of the Community. They are also useful in speeding up the process of cooperation among the partner states.

One of the differences between the EACT and other treaties is that the EACT provides for cooperation among the partner states in the political as well as the economic, social and cultural fields. In contrast, the Economic Community of West African States (ECOWAS) is limited to economic, social and cultural activities.

In Article 151, the EACT recognises Annexes and Protocols as part and parcel of the Treaty. Protocols are concluded in each area of cooperation. Generally, they spell out the objectives, scope of, and institutional mechanisms for cooperation and integration. Protocols are approved by the Heads of State Summit on the recommendation of the Council of Ministers (made up of the ministers responsible for EAC affairs of the partner states) and are subject to signature and ratification by the partner states.

The "hierarchy of laws" in the EAC runs from the EACT to Protocols (and their Annexes) to resolutions, Bills and Acts legislated by the East African Legislative Assembly and finally to regulations. To operationalise each Treaty Protocol, there is a framework of regulations and rules. It is within this framework that either the Summit or the Council of Ministers makes declarations and/or directives. The declarations are meant to confirm that the Summit has a shared opinion and frame of mind on the subject. Declarations are also made as a substitute for an expression of commitment. Directives on the other hand are firm instructions meant to yield action. Recently, the Summit has made directives to support the EAC Secretariat in enforcement of implementation of previous decisions (as at April 2012, these stood at about 500 pieces) not implemented by the partner states. Table 2.2 shows the status of various decision-making instruments of the EAC.

The East African Legislative Assembly (EALA) is the recognised law-making body of the EAC. The EALA is constituted under Chapter Nine of the EACT, Articles 48 to 65. Its membership consists of 45 elected members, nine from each partner state, plus seven ex officio members. The ex officio members include the ministers responsible for EAC affairs of the partner states, their deputies or assistants, the Secretary-General and the Counsel to the Community and the Clerk of the Assembly.

Table 2.2 Decision-making tools and their legal effect

Decision-making organ	Type of instrument	Role of decision-making organ (if any)	Legal effect – binding nature of decision
Summit	Protocols	Must be approved by the Summit. Approval is achieved by consensus.	Binding on partner states and all EAC organs after ratification by all partner states. However, if a protocol is adopted but has not been ratified, it becomes a source of soft law (not binding but highly persuasive); for example, the Environment Protocol and the Kiswahili Commission Protocol have not been ratified by Tanzania.
	Directives	Summit may issue directives; however, most "department" directives tend to be issued by the Council of Ministers.	Binding
	Regulations	Can issue; however, these are the preserve of the Council of Ministers.	Can be binding, though the binding status of regulations is contentious.
	Decisions	Approves decisions from the Council of Ministers.	Are considered binding.
	Declarations	Preserve of the Summit. Used to direct the Secretariat to perform some functions.	Are lowest in the "hierarchy of laws". Do not have any binding force but are highly persuasive (soft law).
	Resolutions	Tend to be directed at the partner states. Also made at the Assembly. Usually tend to have some sort of implementation in practice.	Binding
	Policies	Provide clarification as to how certain instruments should be implemented or how particular pieces of the EAC legislation should be enforced.	They are not binding and have no legal force.
Council of Ministers	Protocols	Verifies Protocols and agrees on forwarding to the Summit. Decisions by consensus. There is a Protocol on decision-making by the Council, passed in the early 2000s that provides for when there is a conflict in provisions.	Binding
	Directives	Directives issued by the Council of Ministers are of the same nature as those passed by the Summit. In practice, the Council of Ministers has used delegated powers to issue directives.	Binding
	Regulations	Has power to issue regulations.	These are somewhat contentious. A decision by the East African Court of Justice ruled that regulations were binding. However, an alternative school of thought believes regulations must be ratified by partner states. The consensus in the European Union (EU) is that both regulations and directives are binding on EU partner states.
	Decisions	Passes decisions on, for example, regional instruments.	Are considered binding.
	Resolutions	Passes resolutions directed at the Secretariat as a follow-up mechanism.	Binding
	Policies	It is the main policy organ on matters such as peace and security, human resources management, etc.	They are not binding and have no legal force.

Apart from the Customs Union and the Common Market, some of the other protocols that have been ratified so far are:

- Environment and Natural Resources Management Protocol;

- Protocol for the Sustainable Development of the Lake Victoria Basin;

- Peace and Security Protocol;

- Protocol on Combating Drug Trafficking in the East African Region;

- Protocol on Standardisation, Quality Assurance, Metrology and Testing;

- Protocol on Foreign Policy Coordination; and

- Protocol on Establishment of a Civil Aviation Safety and Security Oversight Agency.

2.1.3 Policy priorities in the EAC

Various articles of the EACT specify the areas of cooperation (Chapter 11 to 20), which in turn guide policies. The areas of cooperation are a key pillar driving integration. Joint activities and programmes are carried out in specific areas of cooperation. The EACT defines cooperation as the undertaking by the partner states in common, jointly or in concert, of activities in furtherance of the objectives of the Community as provided for under the Treaty or under any contract or agreement made in relation to the objectives of the Community.

The policy priorities of the Community therefore logically flow from the areas of cooperation as stated in the Treaty. In the area of trade liberalisation, for instance, the priorities include the establishment of the following:

- East African Trade Regime (Article 74);

- Customs Union (Article 75); and

- Common Market (Article 76).

In concrete terms, the EAC has used development strategies to plan for implementation of its policy priorities. The first EAC Development Strategy was implemented between 1997 and 2000. Broadly, the strategy had the objective of transforming East Africa into a single market and investment area.

The second EAC Development Strategy was formulated and implemented between 2001 and 2005. Its key priorities were:

- Establishing a Customs Union and a Common Market;

- Building supply capacity in the region with an emphasis on enhancing the capacity of the productive sectors;

- Coordinating macro-economic policies and economic reform; and

- Mobilising resources for investment projects.

The current strategy, whose theme is "Deepening and Accelerating Integration", puts emphasis on the consolidation of a fully-fledged Customs Union through, among others, the development and implementation of the EAC Customs Strategy and harmonisation and simplification of customs procedures. It also envisages full implementation of the Common Market Protocol (CMP). The strategies to achieve this include "approximation and harmonisation of national laws, policies and systems of the partner states to conform to the CMP". On political federation, the aim is to lay the foundation for the federation.

2.2 EAC organs and institutions

2.2.1 The composition and legal basis of key organs

Chapters 2–10 of the EACT establish the institutions of the EAC and describe their functions. All institutions of the EAC therefore derive their legitimacy and authority from the EACT.

The objective of the Community is to develop policies and programmes aimed at widening and deepening cooperation among the partner states in political, economic, social and cultural fields, research and technology, defence, security, and legal and judicial affairs, to their mutual benefit.

Figure 2.1 The structure of the EAC

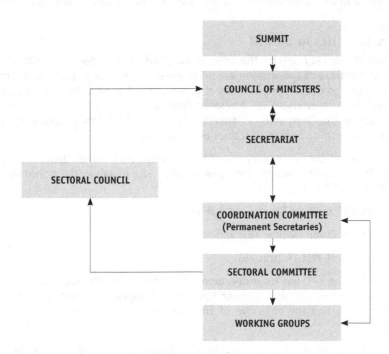

In order to realise its mandate, the Community establishes a number of organs as follows:

- The Heads of State Summit;
- The Council of Ministers;
- The Coordinating Committee;
- Sectoral Councils and Committees;
- The East African Court of Justice;
- The East African Legislative Assembly;
- The Secretariat; and
- Such other organs as may be established by the Summit.

The EAC has also established a number of autonomous and specialised institutions to undertake some of its functions. These institutions are established by the Summit under Article 9(2) of the Treaty and include:

- Lake Victoria Basin Commission;

- East African Science and Technology Commission;

- East African Health Research Commission;

- East African Kiswahili Commission;

- East African Community Civil Aviation Safety and Security Oversight Agency (CASSOA);

- Inter-University Council for East Africa (IUCEA);

- Lake Victoria Fisheries Organisation (LVFO); and

- East African Development Bank (EADB).

2.2.2 The Summit

The Heads of State Summit consists of the heads of state or government of the partner states. There is provision for seconding a minister in the event a head of state or government is unable to attend a particular meeting. The Summit gives general direction to the development and achievement of the objectives of the Community. It meets twice a year (in March/April and November) to consider the annual progress reports and other reports submitted to it by the Council. Extraordinary meetings are held as necessary. Importantly, the Summit also reviews the state of peace, security and good governance within the Community and the progress achieved towards political federation. The Treaty allows the Summit to delegate the exercise of any of its functions to one of its members, the Council or the Secretary-General of the EAC. The power of delegation, however, does not extend to the following core functions:

- Giving of general directions and impetus;

- Appointment of judges to the East African Court of Justice;

- Admission of new members;

- Granting of observer status to foreign countries; and

- Assent to Bills.

The Treaty also empowers the Summit to make rules and orders to guide and direct operations of the Community. Rules are published in the Gazette. The rules come into force on the date of publication. Apart from decisions arising from meetings of the Summit, the Heads of State also assent to Bills emanating from the EALA.

Article 12 of the Treaty provides for meetings of the Summit. The meetings are chaired on a rotational basis and the agenda is determined by the Council. There is no provision for direct participation by non-members. A chairperson serves for a period of one year. Decisions of the Summit are reached by consensus.

2.2.3 The Council of Ministers

The Council of Ministers is the policy organ of the Community. Article 13 defines the membership of the Council: it draws its membership from the ministers responsible for regional cooperation of each partner state and such other ministers as determined by each partner state. Among its functions is to promote, monitor and keep under constant review the implementation of the programmes of the Community. In order to achieve this, it:

- Makes policy decisions;

- Initiates and submits Bills to the Assembly;

- Makes staff rules and regulations; and

- Makes financial rules and regulations.

Other important functions are:

- Submitting annual progress reports to the Summit;
- Preparing the agenda for the meetings of the Summit;
- Implementing the decisions and directives of the Summit;
- Considering measures that should be taken by partner states in order to promote the attainment of the objectives of the Community;
- Considering the budget of the Community; and
- Giving directions to the partner states and to all other organs and institutions of the Community other than the Summit, Court and the Assembly.

As the policy organ of the Community, the Council is the EAC's most powerful body after the Summit. One could say that the Council is the engine of the integration process. It is clear that the Council not only sets the legislative agenda of the Community through initiation of Bills, but also determines what is transacted by the Summit. It gives direction to all the other organs but particularly so the sectoral councils and committees. It also sets up these lower-level organs. However, the Treaty also allows members of EALA to present Private Members' Bills.

To undertake its functions, the Council meets in regular sessions, at least twice a year, one of which is held immediately preceding a meeting of the Summit. Extraordinary meetings are held as necessary. The work of the Council is facilitated by sectoral councils established on a need basis by the Council. Decisions of sectoral councils have the same effect as those of the Council. It also establishes sectoral committees for the same purpose. It is noteworthy that organisations with observer status may attend the opening and closing sessions of Council meetings.

Role of the Council of Ministers

The Council plays a very important role in setting the agenda of discussion by the Summit. It is one of the most powerful organs of the EAC. This is important for civil society organisations aiming to influence the decisions of the Summit. Remember that a majority of decisions of the Summit are made long before the Summit sits, since there will have been a lot of consultation before the Summit meets. One must therefore be clear about the importance of influencing the deliberations before decisions are formally made by the Summit.

2.2.4 The Coordination Committee

The Coordination Committee consists of the permanent secretaries responsible for regional cooperation in each partner state and such other permanent secretaries as each partner state may deem necessary. It reports to the Council of Ministers and is responsible for:

- Submitting reports and recommendations to the Council;
- Implementing decisions of the Summit and the Council of Ministers;
- Determining its own procedures for convening meetings; and
- Requesting a Sectoral Committee to investigate a matter.

2.2.5 Sectoral committees

The Council of Ministers has powers to create sectoral committees. The committees oversee implementation of programmes of the Community in particular sectors. They report to the Coordination Committee and are responsible for:

- Preparing implementation programmes;
- Setting priorities with respect to their respective sectors;
- Monitoring the implementation of programmes in respect to their sectors; and
- Submitting reports and recommendations to the Coordinating Committee.

Sectoral committee members comprise senior officials from sector ministries in the partner states. Technical work is a preserve of these lower-level organs. It is this work that eventually results in decisions of the Community.

Currently, the following 16 Sectoral Councils exist within the EAC institutional framework:

- Sectoral Council on Agriculture and Food Security;
- Sectoral Council on Cooperation in Defence;
- Sectoral Council on Education, Science and Technology, Culture and Sports;
- Sectoral Council on Energy;
- Sectoral Council on Environment and Natural Resources;
- Sectoral Council on Finance and Economic Affairs;
- Sectoral Council on Foreign Policy Coordination;
- Sectoral Council on Gender, Youth, Children, Social Protection and Community Development;
- Sectoral Council on Health;
- Sectoral Council on Interstate Security;
- Sectoral Council on Legal and Judicial Affairs;
- Sectoral Council on Ministers Responsible for EAC Affairs and Planning;
- Sectoral Council on the Monetary Union;
- Sectoral Council on Trade, Industry, Finance and Investment;
- Sectoral Council on Tourism and Wildlife Management; and
- Sectoral Council on Transport, Communications and Meteorology.

It is possible that more sectoral councils will be set up over time to take care of additional aspects of cooperation. It is envisaged, for instance, that a Sectoral Council on Cooperation in Political Matters will be set up, as this is an important area of cooperation. There are also efforts to rationalise the work of sectoral councils to address unnecessary overlaps both in composition and other aspects and make the councils more focused.

2.2.6 The East African Court of Justice

The East African Court of Justice (EACJ) is the judicial organ of the EAC and was established in 2001 under Article 9 of the Treaty. Its mandate is to ensure smooth regional integration through administration of justice and respect for the rule of law. Its jurisdiction encompasses the interpretation and application of the Treaty. It also has jurisdiction to issue advisory opinions and to determine arbitral matters as well as employment and labour disputes that arise between the EAC and its staff. The temporary seat of the EACJ is Arusha until the Summit determines the permanent seat. The High Courts of the partner states serve as sub-registries of the Court. The Principal Judge is resident in Arusha.

The EACJ's jurisdiction encompasses the interpretation and application of the Treaty. The EACJ has jurisdiction to render advisory opinions when requested to do so by the Summit, the Council of Ministers or a partner state. The EACJ also has a mandate to conduct arbitration proceedings when specially called upon to do so by the relevant parties to a contract or by special agreement between the partner states. Furthermore, the EACJ has jurisdiction to entertain employment disputes between the Community (including its organs or institutions) and its employees. The EACJ has further been granted "such other original, appellate, human rights and other jurisdiction as would be determined by the Council of Ministers at a suitable subsequent date".

The human rights jurisdiction for the EACJ remains an area of contention. Human rights jurisdiction is especially important for civil society – various organisations such as the East African Law Society (EALS) and the Independent Medico-Legal Unit have undertaken advocacy in this regard. Granting of explicit human rights jurisdiction has been delayed for the following reasons:

- Partner states already subscribe to the African Charter on Human and Peoples' Rights;

- Human rights jurisdiction should be deferred pending the attainment of a political federation;

- Human rights should remain the primary domain of national jurisdictions; and

- There was a need to clarify the role of national human rights institutions vis-à-vis their potential role in accessing the EACJ as litigants or *amicus curiae*.

In 2004, the EAC Sectoral Council on Legal and Judicial Affairs decided that in view of the scope of the integration process, the jurisdiction of the EACJ should be extended. Subsequently, a draft protocol was prepared for that purpose. The draft was taken through various consultations and reviews between 2005 and 2011. However, when the Council met in 2011, it decided to extend the EACJ's jurisdiction with regard to trade and commercial matters, but excluding original, appellate and human rights matters. This jurisdictional challenge formed the basis of Reference No. 1 of 2010 by the Hon. Sitenda Sebalu. The EACJ in 2011 declared that quick action should be taken to conclude the protocol to operationalise the extended jurisdiction. With more delays in concluding this matter, the EALS filed a case before the EACJ seeking a declaration that the delay in approving the Zero Protocol constituted a violation of the EACT. Subsequently, the case proceeded to the Appellate Division.

In 2012, the EAC Summit of Heads of State overruled the Council by welcoming a resolution of EALA for the amendment of the EACT to extend the jurisdiction of the EACJ to cover among other matters crimes against humanity or conclude the protocol on this matter. This was seen largely as a reaction to the intervention of the International Criminal Court in Kenya indicting suspects in the 2007/2008 post-election violence. In response to this directive, the EAC Council of Ministers requested the EAC Secretariat to prepare a technical paper addressing legal and policy matters regarding universal jurisdiction (including crimes against humanity).

The EALS played a critical role in advocacy on this matter. On comments made in regard to the Revised Protocol to Operationalise the Extended Jurisdiction of the East African Court of Justice, the organisation questioned the apparent desire among the partner states to "redefine and limit the jurisdiction of the Court as recognised by the EACT and reaffirmed by numerous decisions of the EACJ". The organisation also wondered whether depriving the EACJ of all human rights jurisdiction was consistent with efforts to formulate Bills, policies and frameworks focusing on human rights and good governance. However, in November 2013 the Summit extended the EACJ's jurisdiction to cover trade, investment and matters associated with the East African Monetary Union. On human rights and crimes against humanity, the Summit directed the Council of Ministers to work with the African Union (AU).

A number of shortcomings have been pointed out in relation to the EACJ. The most important is that it appears to be under the control of the Summit. It is the Summit that appoints the judges, even though this happens after recommendation by the partner states. Secondly, it is the Summit that decides who among the appointed judges becomes President and/or Vice-President of the Court. Even though the removal of judges from office requires recommendation to the Summit by an ad hoc tribunal, it is the Summit that undertakes the function of appointing the tribunal. The EACT provides that the members of the tribunal thus appointed should consist of judges from the

Commonwealth of Nations. However, it falls short of saying there should be some from outside the partner states to guarantee their independence. Inadequate funding and lack of enforcement of decisions of the EACJ are other weaknesses.

The desire to control the agenda of the EACJ was clearly underscored by amendments to the Treaty on 14 December 2006 and 20 August 2007. These amendments were made in response to a verdict given in *Prof. Peter Anyang Nyong'o and 10 Others vs. The Attorney-General of Kenya and 5 Others*. (Prof. Nyong'o and the other petitioners had challenged the legality of the nomination of nine persons to EALA from Kenya, noting failure to comply with Article 50 of the Treaty.) These amendments included:

- Restructuring the EACJ into two divisions, a First Instance Division and an Appellate Division;

- Adding additional grounds for removing a judge from office;

- Limiting the EACJ's jurisdiction so as not to apply to jurisdiction conferred by the Treaty on organs of partner states;

- Adding a two-month time limit for cases brought by legal and natural persons; and

- Providing grounds for appeal to the Appellate Division of the EACJ.

EAC member states have on several occasions invoked the two-month time limit to challenge the admissibility of human rights cases coming before the EACJ.

It is noteworthy that the Council of Ministers has opposed the extension of the EACJ's jurisdiction to include jurisdiction over the Customs Protocol and the Common Market Protocol. The two protocols have their own dispute settlement mechanisms, undermining the EACJ as the institution that should deal with all disputes between states and EAC institutions to avoid confusion and conflicting rulings.

The EACJ has made rulings that have set a precedent in the matter of jurisdiction. The Katabazi Case of 2007 involved perhaps the worst attack on judicial independence. Paramilitary men, in a show of force, re-arrested 14 Ugandans who had just been granted bail by the High Court of Uganda. The men interfered with preparation of bail papers and took the arrested individuals before a military general court martial. Based on the same facts that had been processed before the High Court, the arrested individuals were charged with unlawful possession of arms and terrorism. A subsequent decision of the Ugandan Constitutional Court ruled the actions unconstitutional; however, the government ignored the ruling, forcing the Ugandan Law Society to petition the EACJ. They argued at the EACJ that the actions of the government, including refusal to obey bail orders, were inconsistent with the EACT. While deciding that it had jurisdiction over the matter, the EACJ decided it would not abdicate from exercising its jurisdiction of interpretation under Article 27(1) merely because the reference includes allegation of human rights violation.

The EALS has petitioned the EACJ on the basis that both the Customs Union and the Common Market Protocol undermined the jurisdiction of the Court. In EACJ Reference No. 1 of 2011, the EALS argued that Article 24(1)(e) of the Customs Union Protocol and Article 54(2) of the Protocol establishing the Common Market were inconsistent with the EACT because they purport to oust the (original) jurisdiction of the EACJ on matters regarding the EAC regional integration processes. The same articles, they further argued, contravened Articles 33(2) and 8(1) and (c) of the Treaty as they purport to grant partner states, national courts, administrative and legal authorities or committees precedence over the EACJ in matters relating to the interpretation and application of the Treaty. The organisation sought several declarations from the Court including, that, "Article 24(1)(e) of the Customs Union Protocol offended Articles 5(1), 8(1)(a) and (c), 27(1), 33(2) and 38(1) and (2) of the Treaty".

2.2.7 The Secretariat
The Secretariat is the executive organ of the Community and therefore the guardian of the Treaty. It is headed by the Secretary-General assisted by Deputy Secretaries-General. It includes the offices of Counsel to the Community and other officers as determined by and appointed by the

Council. As the executive, the Secretariat is in charge of the day-to-day running of the affairs of the Community. It organises meetings of the different organs of the Community and handles official communication with other parties with an interest in the affairs of the Community such as foreign governments. It ensures implementation of regulations and directives of the Council.

The Secretary-General is the principal executive officer, hence the accounting officer of the Community. S/he is also the Secretary of the Summit. S/he is appointed by the Summit upon recommendation by the relevant head of state since the position is rotational. The position is significant in setting the pace of work and culture at the Secretariat as well as of the Community in general. It is also important in determining the priorities of the EAC. It entails a close working relationship with all the organs of the Community for effectiveness.

Article 29(1) gives the Secretary-General immense powers. The Article states as follows:

- Where the Secretary-General considers that a partner state has failed to fulfil an obligation under this Treaty or has infringed a provision of this Treaty, the Secretary-General shall submit his or her findings to the partner state concerned for that partner state to submit its observations on the findings.

The EACT also mandates the Secretary-General through Article 127(4) to provide a forum for consultations between civil society organisations (CSOs), the private sector, other interest groups and appropriate institutions of the Community. To this effect, the Consultative Dialogue Framework for Civil Society and Private Sector is one of the structures set up to enable consultation.

A liaison office for civil society exists within the Secretariat. CSOs have faced challenges working with the office because there is only one officer in charge. Even with organisations that have observer status, complaints have been voiced over the way invitations to meetings are issued, the late presentation of documents leading to inadequate preparation, and other issues that the EAC Secretariat needs to look at to improve participation of civil society in the integration process.

2.2.8 The East African Legislative Assembly

The East African Legislative Assembly (EALA) is the organ set up to legislate on behalf of the Community. Article 48 provides for the membership of EALA. It was inaugurated on 30 November 2001 and comprises 45 members elected from partner states and seven ex officio members. The ex officio members are the ministers in charge of East African Community from each partner state, the Secretary-General and the Counsel to the Community, as well as the Clerk to the Assembly.

EALA's functions encompass the legislative, representative and oversight mandate. Specifically, EALA is mandated to

- Make laws;
- Debate and approve the budget of the Community;
- Consider annual audit reports and annual reports on the activities of the Community;
- Discuss all matters pertaining to the Community; and
- Make recommendations.

The business of EALA is defined by its Bills, motions, petitions and questions. Article 59 of the Treaty gives every member of EALA a right to propose any motion or to introduce any Bill in the Assembly. Rule 64 of the EALA Rules of Procedure (2001) expounds on Article 59. Apart from emphasising a member's right to move a private Bill, it also provides for a Committee of the House to initiate any Bill within its area of competence, and for such Bills to be introduced by the chairperson of the committee. Article 62 provides that enactment of legislation of the Community shall be effected by means of Bills passed by the Assembly and assented to by the Heads of State. When a Bill has been duly passed by the Assembly, the Speaker of the Assembly shall submit the Bill to the Heads of State Summit for assent. The heads of state may assent to or withhold assent to a Bill of the Assembly.

Figure 2.2 Organisation structure of the EAC

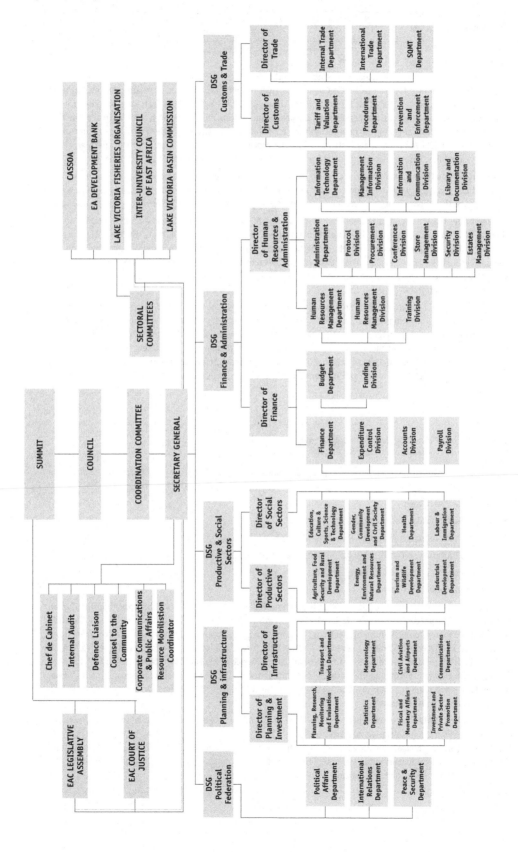

The powers of EALA

EALA makes its own rules and procedures.

Legislative power: Unlike other regional assemblies on the continent, EALA has legislative powers and this has enabled the Community to enact legislation needed to push the integration agenda forward, without the need for recourse to the partner states for ratification. To this end, EALA scrutinises all draft laws proposed by the Council to ensure that they are compatible with the goal of integration and in line with the EAC Treaty. The first Assembly made significant progress in enacting laws for the Community, notably the East African Community Customs Management Act 2004. It also established mechanisms that allowed easy liaison with the partner states' national assemblies, through interparliamentary relations seminars and intercommittee activities.

Budgetary power: This mandate enables EALA to debate the budget and allocate resources according to the priorities of the Community. EALA approves the Community's budget and oversees its implementation. EALA is also charged with the responsibility of considering annual reports of the Audit Commission.

Oversight role: EALA has played this role by interrogating EAC policies and the proper and accountable utilisation of EAC funds. This function is undertaken through EALA's standing committees, whose duties include oversight of the programmes and projects of the Community. The constant contact and dialogue between the committees and the respective departments of the EAC Secretariat are meant to ensure that the road map designed by the EAC is adhered to. EALA to this end seeks regular reports on the implementation of the various programmes and projects.

Representation: EALA serves as the main link between the institutions of the EAC and the people of East Africa. EALA has rotational meetings in the partner states as a way of reaching out to EAC citizens and has also conducted public hearing workshops on the major stages of integration and legislation. In terms of outreach, EALA has striven to market the Community through tours and outreach programmes in different parts of East Africa. At the international level, it has participated in meetings of the Interparliamentary Union, Commonwealth Parliamentary Association, Pan-African Parliament and the African-Caribbean and Pacific–European Union.

The EALA committee system and relationship with civil society

EALA operates through the committee system in accordance with Rule 77 of its rules of procedure. Some of the committees are:

*   Accounts Committee;
*   Legal, Rules and Privileges Committee;
*   Agriculture, Tourism and Natural Resources Committee;
*   Regional Affairs and Conflict Resolution General Purpose Committee;
*   Communication, Trade and Investment Committee; and
*   House Business Committee.

CSOs have worked with various committees on legislation. For instance, Kituo Cha Katiba worked on the Human Rights Bill, and the Eastern African National Networks on AIDS Services Organisations worked on the HIV/AIDS Bill. Advocacy took the form of meetings, presentation of documents, comments on the documents presented, and identifying individual champions for the Bills. There is a lot of scope for working with EALA on the legislative front and learning lessons from what CSOs have achieved. The Consultative Dialogue Framework can enhance this relationship significantly since it brings together the various stakeholder groups. However, attempts to undermine the roles of EALA members by removing their ability to present Private Members' Bills will undermine this relationship.

Since inception, EALA has enacted over 40 Bills, most of them Private Members' Bills. It has won international acclaim for this unique legislative mandate, which sets it apart from similar bodies on the continent, such as ECOWAS and SADC, which are merely advisory and consultative. This mandate has seen EALA pass a record number of laws. Efforts by some member states to deny members the right to move Private Members' Bills started in 2012, but have not so far been successful.

2.2.9 Specialised institutions of the EAC

The Community has several institutions that handle specialised functions (Table 2.3). These institutions generally deal with diverse areas of cooperation. CSOs with an interest in these areas of cooperation may find opportunities for engagement. Those with an interest in aviation safety, for instance, may be able to carry out advocacy work with CASSOA on standards. Those that work with fisher folk around Lake Victoria may seek opportunities to carry out advocacy through the Lake Victoria Basin Commission.

Apart from these institutions, other forums for cooperation between institutions have been developed. The EAC convenes the following:

- EAC Forum of Electoral Commissions;
- EAC Forum of National Human Rights Institutions; and
- Forum for East African Chief Justices

The following independent bodies work closely with the EAC and provide critical forums for engagement with civil society:

- East Africa Association of Anti-Corruption Authorities; and
- East Africa Police Chiefs Cooperating Organisation.

When Kituo Cha Katiba initiated advocacy work on the EAC Bill of Rights, for instance, it engaged strategically with the national human rights institutions in the three initial partner states (Uganda, Kenya and Tanzania). Representatives of these institutions formed the Task Force on the Draft Bill of Rights for the East African Community.

Table 2.3 Institutions of the EAC

Institution	Location	Mission/vision/objectives/mode of operation/achievements
Civil Aviation Safety and Security Oversight Agency (CASSOA)	Entebbe, Uganda	To ensure coordinated development of an effective and sustainable civic aviation safety and security oversight infrastructure in the Community. It works with partner states' civil aviation authorities. A major achievement has been to harmonise regulations and development of guidance materials, which have been promulgated in the partner states.
East African Development Bank (EADB)	Kampala, Uganda	One of the "residual" institutions carried over from the 1967–1977 EAC. It was formed via a charter. Its mandate is to raise resources and provide credit to the private sector. Apart from lending, it also provides advisory services and is a "development partner".
Lake Victoria Basin Commission (LVBC)	Kisumu, Kenya	Established through a protocol to ensure sustainable development and management of the natural resources of the Lake Victoria Basin.
Lake Victoria Fisheries Organisation (LVFO)	Jinja, Uganda	To harmonise national measures for sustainable use of the lake's fisheries resources and to develop and adopt conservation and management measures to achieve that purpose. Aims to provide a forum to discuss initiatives to deal with "environmental conditions and water quality in the Lake Basin, to promote research with respect to the living resources of the lake, and to address problems of non-indigenous species" (EAC, 2012).
The Inter-University Council for East Africa (IUCEA)	Kampala, Uganda	To encourage and develop mutually beneficial collaboration between member universities, governments and other public and private organisations. Aims "to meet regional development needs and undertake resolution of issues in every appropriate sector of the activity of higher education" (EAC, 2012).

2.3 Decision-making at the EAC

2.3.1 General basis for decision-making

EAC decisions are made by the key organs established by the EACT. It is worth noting from the outset that decisions of the EAC are made by consensus. This means if one partner state opposes a decision, it is binding on all partner states. This creates challenges when some states are not comfortable with some issues. Indeed, some decisions regarding the fast-tracking of the Political Federation, when to finalise and implement the Monetary Union Protocol and others, were delayed because of the inability to reach consensus on specific issues. Most notably, in 2012, Kenya, Uganda and Rwanda used the principle of variable geometry to make decisions binding on the three states, which entered into a so-called Coalition of the Willing. The main reason for the "tripartite" approach was to enable these states to move cooperation forward on issues that seemed to unsettle Tanzania and Burundi and which therefore could not be agreed on consensually.

The EAC organs hold periodic meetings that enable them to make decisions. Their effect on programmes and other activities of the EAC depends on the level of the decision-making structure. Usually, decisions of a higher level structure will be binding on lower level entities. Decisions of the Summit, for instance, will be binding on the Council of Ministers. The extent to which decisions are binding therefore depends on the hierarchy of organs of the EAC. The following instruments, among others, create decision-making structures and give direction to decision-making processes:

- *EACT*: The Treaty defines the different roles of the organs – the Summit, the Council of Ministers, the Coordinating Committee, and so on. These organs all have different decision-making powers.

- *Protocols*: These are agreements that augment the EACT. Protocols are made in line with the EACT; their provisions cannot contravene the Treaty. They deal with specific areas of cooperation such as trade, land, setting up the Customs Union, Common Market, etc. Protocols also create bodies that deal with specific issues. These bodies exercise decision-making powers in regard to the areas with which they deal.

- *Development Plans*: The programmes of the EAC rely on Strategic Plans that are developed and reviewed regularly. These plans contain important road maps on specific issues and enable efforts to be channelled.

The East African Community Treaty

As the main legal document of the Community, the Treaty establishes the legal basis for decision-making in the following ways:

- By setting up the institutions and organs of the Community such as the Summit. The different organs set up by the EACT have different decision-making capacities, which are also in line with their functions. As the main decision-making organ, the Summit's decisions are binding on all the other organs. In fact, it is the decisions of the Summit that set the tempo for the roles and decision-making capacity of the other organs. Usually, the Summit will issue directives to the other organs in order to implement their decisions.

- By establishing the objectives (Article 5), the fundamental principles (Article 6), and the operational principles (Article 7). One of the most important operational principles of the Community is "people-centredness". All decisions and programmes of the Community are to be guided by this principle. It is arguable that decisions of the Community can be challenged on the basis of how people-centred they are.

- By defining the legal capacity of the Community. This is achieved by Article 4 which proclaims as follows:

- The Community shall have the capacity, within each of the partner states, of a body corporate with perpetual succession, and shall have power to acquire, hold, manage and dispose of land and other property, and to sue and be sued in its own name.

- This provision is important since it gives real power to the Community and its organs to make decisions and undertake transactions in the territories of the partner states without facing legal challenges.

- By defining the nature, type and scope of cooperation by thematic areas, which is done through Chapters 11 to 27 of the Treaty. Organs of the Community are structured to enable decision-making about cooperation in the identified thematic areas. Some of the themes of cooperation are:

  - Trade liberalisation and development;

  - Investment and industrial development;

  - Standardisation, quality assurance, metrology and testing;

  - Monetary and financial cooperation;

  - Cooperation in infrastructure and services; and

  - Enhancing the role of women in socio-economic development – a progressive theme because the communities within the EAC remain largely patriarchal.

- By establishing procedures for decision-making that include setting up schedules of meetings for the different organs and procedures of establishing Protocols and other relevant undertakings. A relevant illustration here is Article 151, which gives the criteria for establishing Protocols by proclaiming as follows:

  - The partner states shall conclude such Protocols as may be necessary in each area of cooperation, which shall spell out the objectives and scope of, and institutional mechanisms for cooperation and integration.

2.3.2 Decision-making in practice

Protocols of the EAC

We have already pointed out that Protocols of the EAC are also instruments of decision-making. A Protocol supplements, amends or qualifies the Treaty. The passage of Protocols requires national consultations in partner states. Such consultations involve stakeholders such as civil society and the private sector.

The supplemental role of a Protocol is important because the Treaty cannot define all things about the Community. If this were to be attempted, the Treaty would have many thousands of pages.

The most important way that Protocols promote decision-making is by establishing bodies other than those already established by the Treaty.

Apart from setting up other bodies responsible for decision-making and their functions, Protocols also set out specific actions that need to be taken by the contracting parties to facilitate realisation of the objectives of integration. For instance, the Common Market Protocol under Article 16 on Trade Facilitation required partner states to initiate trade facilitation by reducing the number and volume of documentation required in respect of trade among the partner states. This provision creates the basis for decision-making by the partner states in this specific area.

Decision-making in the EAC in practice proceeds something like this: either partner states or the EAC Secretariat may initiate an issue that requires policy direction. After the initial drafting, an expert group is constituted to examine the issue. The experts, mainly representatives of diverse ministries and sectors from the partner states, then give their views to the Secretariat, which prepares an amended draft for presentation to the relevant Sectoral Committee. The Sectoral Committee then considers the relevance, acceptability and applicability of the policy prescription. Discussions on budgetary implications of the policy are discussed by the Coordinating Committee. It is the comments made by the Coordinating Committee that largely determine the actions of the Council of Ministers. This is especially so for issues that require substantial budgetary input. Figure 2.3 is a representation of the decision-making process.

Figure 2.3 The decision-making process

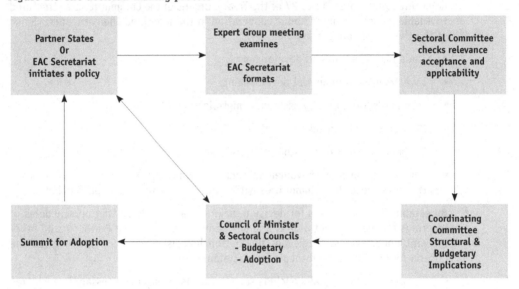

There are various ways in which civil society can influence the decisions of the EAC, as shown in Table 2.5. In order to facilitate decision-making, the organs of the EAC hold various meetings in a given year. The frequency of meetings is already set out by the Treaty for all the organs. Table 2.4 gives a snapshot of the meetings of the different organs.

Table 2.4 Meetings of organs of the EAC

Organ	Frequency of meetings
Summit	At least twice a year, but can have extraordinary sessions/meetings
Council	At least twice a year, one of which is held immediately preceding a meeting of the Summit, and may hold extraordinary meetings as necessary
Coordinating Committee	At least twice a year subject to directions given by the Council, preceding the meetings of the Council; may hold extraordinary meetings at the request of the chairperson
Sectoral Committees	As often as possible to discharge their mandate and subject to directions of Council

Table 2.5 Decision-making processes at the EAC and proposed civil society actions

Level	Current process	Proposed civil society action lines
Partner states or the EAC Secretariat	At this level agenda or decision proposals are introduced by: • A partner state (through its hierarchy); • Department or directorate of the EAC Secretariat; • The Council of Ministers; or • The Summit.	Civil society should: • Work with government departments/ ministries to influence policy/agenda proposals; • Research on and inform formulation and formatting of agenda and policy proposals; and • Organise debate and public fora on key thematic issues to influence agenda and policy proposals.
Expert work groups/ meetings	The current EAC practice is that once an agenda or an item has been proposed and agreed upon, consultants or experts are commissioned to package a policy document that is subjected to experts' scrutiny. These experts include government, civil society and business representatives. The most common shortcomings of expert meetings have been short notice, materials not supplied on time, and too much government direction.	Civil society should insist on: • Reasonable time for meetings; • Advance access to workshop agenda and materials; • Participation in producing materials for workshop discussions; and • Provision of technical support where possible. Civil society should form strong thematic constituencies in order to competently participate in such fora.
Sectoral Committee	The scrutinised and agreed proposals are submitted to the Sectoral Committee.	Civil society should: • Lobby the EAC to be represented at the Sectoral Committee; and • Involve the media on the agenda of the Sectoral Committee with commentaries on the agenda and impact on society.
Coordinating Committee	The policy documents with budgetary recommendations are submitted to the Coordinating Committee and its sub-committees for scrutiny, adoption and recommendation to the Council of Ministers.	Civil society should: • Prior to the Coordinating Committee meeting, seek meetings with representatives to these committees at the national government level and make appropriate submissions. • Seek to hold its own sectoral coordinating meeting alongside the EAC government session to generate comments to be shared with the Coordinating Committee. • Before the Coordinating Committee submits protocol, policy or decision proposals to the Council of Ministers, solicit written comments or proposals from civil society.
Council of Ministers	The recommendations of the Coordinating Committee that require the Council of Ministers' attention are submitted to the Council for review and adoption.	Civil society should seek audience with the Council of Ministers to make its position known on each decision, policy or protocol proposal submitted to them.
The Summit	Once the proposals are approved and adopted by the Council of Ministers, where necessary, they will be sent to the Summit for adoption. The Summit will then: • Direct the EAC Secretariat to implement policy; or • Return the document (if Protocol) to the Council of Ministers for ratification; or • Return to the Council of Ministers if rejected.	Civil society should: • Put in place appropriate monitoring and review mechanisms to follow up on policy and protocol implementation; • Mobilise its membership in implementation of the policy/Protocol; and • Work with EAC and partner states to restart negotiations on rejected proposals or protocols.

2.3.3 Decision-making by the Summit

The Summit is the top decision-making body in the EAC. Before it meets to take decisions, many processes will already have been concluded by the lower-level organs. It is the activities of the other three organs that inform the decisions of the Summit. It is worth noting that decision-making by the Summit is enabled by the suggestions made by the Council of Ministers.

Decisions regarding fast-tracking the political federation

During the Special Summit of 27–29 August 2004, the Heads of State made the declaration on fast-tracking the Political Federation of East Africa and established the Committee on Fast-Tracking the East African Federation. This Committee was chaired by the then Attorney-General of the Republic of Kenya, Amos Wako. The aim of the Committee given through a communiqué of the Special Summit on 28 August 2004, was, "to examine ways and means to expedite and compress the process of integration so that the ultimate goal of a Political Federation is achieved through a fast-track mechanism". The committee submitted its report to the Summit in November 2004. It recommended that the Political Federation be established by 2013.

When they met again in an Extraordinary Summit in May 2005, the Heads of State received and considered the *Report of the Committee on Fast-Tracking East African Federation*. Subsequently, they established the post of Deputy Secretary-General in charge of coordinating the process of fast-tracking the federation. Because of the widespread desire expressed by citizens to understand the federation concept better, they also directed the establishment of national consultative mechanisms for wider consultations with the East African people. These consultations were held between October 206 and June 2007.

At the Extraordinary Summit held in August 2007 in Arusha, the Heads of State further directed that steps be taken to expedite the establishment of the Common Market by 2010 and the Monetary Union by 2012 in preparation for the political federation. Subsequently, the Common Market was launched on 1 July 2010 and the Protocol for the establishment of the Monetary Union was developed by the end of 2012. However, the signing of the protocol was delayed.

2.3.4 Decision-making by the Council of Ministers

As the main policy-making organ of the EAC, the Council is at the centre of the decision-making process. Both the Sectoral Committees and the Coordination Committee are answerable to the Council. The Council gives both bodies directions in undertaking their decision-making roles. Of more significance, the Council determines the issues that are considered by the Summit when it meets. To facilitate this, it meets before every Summit meeting. Meetings of the Council therefore have a lot of significance for all stakeholders of the EAC.

The Council plays a critical role in decision-making. It assigns duties to all the bodies beneath it in the decision-making chain and makes specific requests to the Summit in terms of decisions that need to be made.

The decisions of the Summit and the Council are usually gazetted by the Secretariat. Such gazette notices can be found on the website of the EAC (www.eac.int).

Decisions of the Council regarding the East African Customs Management Bill

During the 12th Ordinary Meeting of 25 August 2006, the Council:

- Considered and adopted the Bill entitled the East African Community Customs Management (Amendment) Bill, 2006; and
- Referred the aforesaid Bill to the Sectoral Council on Legal and Judicial Affairs for consideration.

	Decisions made regarding the EAC/SADC/COMESA Tripartite Summit

During the 15th ordinary meeting held on 17–18 March 2008 in Arusha, the Council:

- Took note of the proposed Common Market for Eastern and Southern Africa (COMESA)/EAC/SADC Tripartite Summit to consider issues of strategic importance to the integration of the eastern and southern African region both regionally and globally, including infrastructure development, trade, peace and security and investments in energy;
- Requested the Summit to pronounce itself on the need for the Tripartite Summit of SADC, COMESA and the EAC;
- Directed the Secretariat to consult COMESA and SADC on the most appropriate date for the proposed Tripartite Summit; and
- Directed the Secretariat to consult and get inputs from the partner states in the development of technical papers for the proposed Tripartite Summit.

2.3.5 The Calendar of Activities

The EAC Calendar of Activities contains details of all activities undertaken by the EAC. Usually, for each event, the calendar gives the following details: date, organ or institution of the EAC that is responsible; the activity and its objective; expected output; sources of funding; who is to participate; venue; and justification.

Table 2.6 shows activities in the July to December 2012 Calendar.

The calendar of activities is found on the website of the EAC (www.eac.int). It is a useful tool for civil society participation in the affairs of the Community.

Table 2.6 Calendar of Activities July to December 2012 – select activities

Date	Organ/institution	Activity/meeting	Objective
23–27 July 2012	C & T	1st EAC steering committee meeting on the 13th EAC *Jua Kali/Nguvu Kazi* Exhibition	Preparations for the 13th EAC *Jua Kali/Nguvu Kazi* exhibition
27–31 August 2012	Legal	25th Ordinary Meeting of the Council of Ministers	To make policy decisions and review implementation of Council decisions
24–28 September 2012	EAC Secretariat	8th Ordinary Meeting of the EAC Sectoral Council of Ministers of Health	Strengthen EAC regional cooperation and integration in the health sector
8–12 October 2012	EAC Secretariat	Meeting of the EAC Regional Steering Committee for the 4th Annual EAC Health and Scientific Conference	Preparations for the 4th Annual EAC Health and Scientific Conference
30 November 2012		14th Summit Meeting	
25 November–7 December 2012	EALA	Convene 2nd Meeting of the 1st Session of the 3rd Assembly	To debate and adopt resolutions, motions and committee reports, ask questions and follow up action on key decisions

2.3.6 Opportunities for engagement

Different organisations have used different fora to engage with the EAC. Some have been granted observer status while others have signed specific memoranda of understanding (MoUs) with the Secretariat. Below we outline some of the ways that have been used by civil society to participate in decision-making.

Observer status

The rules of Observer Status provide the framework for granting observer status to CSOs, intergovernmental organisations and governments. Observer status guarantees observer organisations an opportunity to attend meetings of the organs of the Community, provide input on subjects that concern them and reply to questions directed at them. However, it has been observed that the rules are very limiting for civil society. For instance, they require that organisations applying for observer status be registered in all five member states of the EAC.

Memoranda of understanding

Other organisations have used more innovative ways, for example through MoUs. The Eastern African Subregional Support Initiative for the Advancement of Women (EASSI) used this approach to advocate for the draft EAC Protocol on Gender Equality. This avenue for engagement is said to be more appropriate for service provision agencies aiming to supplement the efforts of the EAC at local, national and regional levels.

The EAC Consultative Dialogue Framework for Civil Society and Private Sector

The Framework provides for national and regional dialogues through the national ministries in charge of the EAC (national dialogue) and the EAC Secretariat (regional dialogue). The Framework recognises the East African Civil Society Organisations Forum (EACSOF) as the platform for civil society participation and the East Africa Business Council for private sector organisations. At the end of each year, the Secretary-General's Forum for civil society and private sector brings together the different stakeholders at a meeting that makes resolutions on issues of importance to the stakeholders. These resolutions are then passed on to the Council of Ministers.

Advocacy through EALA

Organisations such as Kituo cha Katiba and the East Africa Network of National AIDS Support Organisations (EANNASO) have taken part in drafting legislation and have been able to advocate for their passage in EALA. These organisations have largely worked with private members through Private Members' Bills. There is a great deal of opportunity and potential to work with EALA, especially if attempts by some member states to undermine EALA's Private Member's Bills do not succeed.

Litigation through EACJ

Organisations with a legal and human rights mandate, such as the East Africa Law Society and Independent Medical Legal Unit, have so far successfully used the EACJ a as an avenue for advocacy, particularly on human rights issues. Interpretation of the Treaty has enabled the development of jurisprudence in the EAC. There is an opportunity in this area for more interventions aimed at constructing a positive, people- and human rights-friendly jurisprudence.

Expert working groups

CSOs with particular expertise have joined working groups on some of the major issues of cooperation such as security. For example, the Africa Policing Civilian Oversight Forum has been providing technical support in the development of the EAC Standard Operating Procedures on Policing in East Africa. Participation in working groups requires a close relationship with the EAC. This can partly be provided through EACSOF under the EAC Consultative Dialogue Framework for Civil Society and Private Sector. The importance of working groups is that they provide the raw material through which the higher-level decision-making institutions conduct their affairs.

Cross-border initiatives

A number of organisations are involved in cross-border activities aimed at supporting sustainable development across borders of partner states, since border communities face certain unique challenges brought about by the realities of integration. The initiatives therefore promote regional "people to people" cooperation for sustainable development. The Centre for Law and Research International therefore launched a cross-border intervention at the Taveta/Holili border by looking at the status of implementation of the Holili Border Agreement of 9 October 2012 on the relaxation of border controls at Kenya/Tanzania border points to enable free movement of goods, services and residents in line with the Customs Union Protocol and the Common Market Protocol.

2.4 Budgets and financing of EAC activities

2.4.1 General information on budgets and budgeting

In order to undertake its programmes, the EAC receives funding from member states and contributions from donors. The Treaty provides the basic requirements regarding the budget. Budgets are done every year for the organs and institutions of the Community. The Secretary-General is in overall charge of budget preparation. The budgets are approved by EALA upon recommendation by the Council of Ministers. Traditionally, it is the chair of the Council who tables the budget in EALA.

Partner states make equal contributions to the Community's budget. The Treaty creates opportunity for the Community to receive donations from "regional" and "international" sources and any other sources as determined by the Council. Other possible resources are defined as grants, donations, funds for projects and programmes and technical assistance, as well as income earned from the activities of the Community. The Community's financial year runs from 1 July to 30 June, which is the same as the financial year of the partner states.

2.4.2 The budgeting cycle

The budgeting cycle starts with pre-budget conferences during which key funding priorities are determined.

The pre-budget conference for the 2013/2014 financial year, for example, was held from 15 to 17 August 2012 in Arusha, Tanzania. Some of the priorities discussed during the conference were:

- Establishing a single customs territory including the necessary legal and administrative frameworks to manage the territory and complete elimination of customs-related non-tariff barriers (NTBs);

- The progressive implementation of the Common Market Protocol, by putting in place the necessary legal and institutional frameworks and closely monitoring implementation;

- Establishing the Grand Free Trade Area comprising 28 African countries under the Tripartite EAC–COMESA–SADC Initiative, signalling the importance placed on the continent-wide integration process;

- Implementing the EAC Food Security and Climate Change Master Plan and the EAC Industrialisation Strategy; and

- Undertaking the activities of the Lake Victoria Basin Commission (LVBC).

The budget estimates for the 2012/2013 financial year totalled USD 138,316,455. In terms of expenditure, this amount was spread as shown in Table 2.7. The breakdown in Table 2.8 shows the sources and proportion of funds estimated to be given by different sources in accordance with the Budget Speech.

The partner states are required to remit their contributions to the EAC accounts by December. Funds from donors are only factored into the budgeting process once the financing agreements have been signed and funds committed.

The EAC budgeting cycle in five steps
1. August–September: Pre-budget conference to work on the global priorities for funding in the coming financial year
2. October–December: EAC organs and institutions work on their budget proposals
3. January: The Finance and Administration (F&A) Committee meets to consider the budget proposals
4. March–April: Council of Ministers meets to consider, adopt and table the budget in EALA for debate and approval
5. April–June: Partner states incorporate their share of the budget in their national budgeting process.

Table 2.7 Distribution of the 2012/2013 financial year budget

Item	Amount (in USD)	Percentage
East African Community Secretariat	68,339,098	49.40
East African Legislative Assembly	12,511,772	9.04
East African Court of Justice	4,117,210	2.97
Lake Victoria Basin Commission	40,039,716	28.94
Inter-University Council for East Africa	10,105,618	7.30
Lake Victoria Fisheries Organisation	3,203,041	2.31
Total	138,316,455	100

Source: EAC Budget Speech, 2012/2013

Table 2.8 Sources and estimated proportion per source for 2012/2013

Item	Amount (in USD)	Percentage
Partner states' contributions through the ministries responsible for EAC affairs	35,375,722	25.57
Partner states through other agencies	4,825,709	3.49
Development partners' support	97,079,329	70.18
Other income	1,035,695	0.75
Total	138,316,455	100

Source: EAC Budget Speech, 2012/2013

Funding by donors

Table 2.8 shows that the contribution expected from donors for 2012/2013 amounted to more than 70% of the budget. The expected donor contribution was therefore almost three times the contribution by partner states.

The fact that the EAC relies heavily on donor funds raises questions as to the interests that inform the integration process. It is possible for the donor institutions and governments to use financial resources as a way of controlling the agenda of the EAC. Thus the EAC is likely to embrace interests other than those of the populations of the EAC.

Funding by partner states

The contribution of the partner states during for 2012/2013 amounted to just over 29% (contributions through ministries in charge of EAC affairs and through other agencies) of the budget. Suggestions to increase the funding levels by partner states and reduce dependency on donors have included suggestions that the funding system be restructured so that partner states give funding in proportion to either their GDP or overall revenue collection. In line with this approach, bigger economies like Kenya (GDP about USD 30 billion) would contribute more than smaller economies like Burundi (GDP about USD 2.33 billion). However, this was countered by concerns that it would create an unequal relationship between the partner states.

In the latest development on this front, from June 2014, the bloc had planned to introduce a new import levy to finance the Secretariat's budget. The proposed 1% levy will be an additional charge on the existing import taxes. According to *The East African* newspaper, the total value of EAC imports from outside the region amounted to USD 34.29 billion in 2012; therefore, the Secretariat could collect up to USD 342.9 million from the levy. The proposal, which was approved by the EAC Council of Ministers and recommended to the Heads of State Summit in November 2013, was expected to have been approved during the EAC Ordinary Summit scheduled in Nairobi in April 2014, but unfortunately was shot down at the last minute. The new funding mechanism would have enabled the EAC to more than meet its budget, still largely funded by donors. The proposed 2014/2015 budget stands at USD 134 million.

EAC Partnership Fund

The EAC Partnership Fund is a donor-funding mechanism that funds EAC projects and programmes. The Fund was set up to promote implementation of the EACT, with a view to:

- Enhancing regional integration and socio-economic development;
- Facilitating planning and accounting of Development Partners Funds; and
- Encouraging Development Partners and the EAC to jointly contribute to the Fund to ensure availability of funds for activities.

Table 2.9 shows the amounts the fund disbursed from 2006/2007 to 2011/2012.

Table 2.9 Disbursements by the EAC Partnership Fund (USD million)

Financial Year	Budget	Disbursement
FY 2006/2007	1.74	0.65
FY 2007/2008	3.6	1.9
FY 2008/2009	7.7	6.1
FY 2009/2010	8.8	6.2
FY 2010/2011	8.1	8.0
FY 2011/2012	6.1	5.1

Source: EAC Resource Mobilisation Office

2.4.3 Points of influence

The pre-budget conferences create an opportunity for civil society to take part in the budgeting process. It is at this point that budget priorities are determined. However, the prioritisation process also takes into account the priorities as set out in the Development Strategies. It is therefore crucial for civil society to be acquainted with those priorities.

It is important to influence the Development Strategies since they set long-term priorities, which in turn determine where funding goes. This can only be achieved if civil society representatives understand EAC processes and are ready to engage from a point of knowledge.

It is useful to know which donors fund 70.18% of the budget and what interests they represent. This could open up other avenues of influencing not only the budget but also the priorities set out in the Development Strategies.

Funding is channelled to different institutions of the EAC according to the Budget Speech. An idea of which institutions are funded and for what purpose is useful. This will, for instance, facilitate the work of organisations interested in ensuring accountability in management of resources by the different organs and institutions of the EAC.

Organisations interested in accountability in management of resources could also use the information on achievements recorded in prior financial years as is reflected in the budget speeches.

2.5 Relationship with the AU and other RECs

The EAC has observer status with the AU and the Secretary-General is invited to all AU Summits. In 2012, the EAC posted a liaison officer to the AU. The AU also has a liaison officer at the EAC Secretariat. The liaison office is meant to formalise the relationship between the EAC and AU, informing the AU of what is happening at the EAC and vice versa. The liaison officer deals mainly with peace and security issues in line with the AU's mandate of enabling regional economic communities to deal with instability and manage conflicts.

CSOs have pointed out some shortcomings in this arrangement, particularly the capacity of the liaison offices. The liaison offices are held and run by one person on each side. The AU and the EAC are both large organisations with multiple meetings and events. It is therefore difficult for the liaison officer to report effectively on all developments.

The EAC and the AU have a close working relationship in the areas of reconstruction and conflict management due to the understanding that the neighbours should play the greatest role in ensuring stability within RECs. For example, on issues such as troop contributions, the AU tries to encourage countries to get contributions from within the EAC member states when there is a conflict in East Africa. In the African Union Mission to Somalia (AMISOM), many of the senior-ranking officials come from EAC partner states (Uganda, Tanzania and Kenya).

2.5.1 Cross-membership of RECs

Overlaps in the membership of RECs may complicate relationships. Some of the EAC partner states also belong to RECs such as COMESA, SADC and Intergovernmental Authority on Development (IGAD). Table 2.10 shows the overlapping membership of the EAC partner states. This only presents the picture as far as the EAC partner states are concerned. The picture for the continent overall is even more complicated.

Overlapping membership of RECs has been cited as a problem in the implementation of the integration agenda at the continental level. The Economic Commission of Africa pointed out that 95% of the members of RECs in Africa belong to another REC. Countries admit that multiple membership makes it difficult for them to meet their obligations to the RECs to which they belong. It also leads to low implementation of programmes.

2.5.2 EAC partner states' role in IGAD

As shown in Table 2.10, Kenya and Uganda are also members of IGAD. IGAD was established in 1996, taking over from the Intergovernmental Authority on Drought and Development established in 1986 with a focus on development and environmental control. Over the years, IGAD has come to be associated more with conflict resolution in the Horn of Africa region. It has played a significant role in the Somalia peace process as a key supporter of the Federal Government of Somalia. With the approval of the AU, for instance, IGAD deployed forces to the IGAD Peace Support Mission to Somalia before it was replaced by the United Nations-sanctioned AMISOM.

Because of its more robust peace and security framework, IGAD is at the forefront of some of the most technical and complex peace and security issues in the region. It has developed protocols to deal with issues such as maritime piracy and counter-terrorism. In fact, the EAC engages the AU on matters of peace and security through IGAD. IGAD has been responsible for some of the missions in which EAC states have taken part, such as deployment of troops in Somalia. Meetings of IGAD, just before the AU Summit, have also enabled the body to influence AU decisions, especially on peace and conflict.

Table 2.10 Participation of EAC partner states in different RECs

EAC	COMESA	IGAD	SADC	ECCAS*	CEN-SAD**
Kenya	Kenya	Kenya			Kenya
Tanzania			Tanzania		
Uganda	Uganda	Uganda			
Rwanda	Rwanda			Rwanda	
Burundi	Burundi			Burundi	

* Economic Community of Central African States

** Community of Sahel-Saharan States

Sources: Various

2.6 Communication

Communications between the EAC and the partner states are handled through the various ministries in charge of EAC affairs. These ministries coordinate all EAC matters at the national level. With the rest of the world (i.e. with governments, donors, etc.), communication is mainly through the Secretary-General, who is the accounting officer of the Community. However, countries are allowed to send representatives/ambassadors to the EAC. Under the rules for observer status, foreign countries can also apply to be observers.

Since RECs have a relationship with the AU as the continental body's building blocks, communications with the AU are handled at the highest level of authority by the Secretary-General.

2.7 Civil society in the EAC

2.7.1 Recognition of civil society in the EAC

The inclusion of civil society in the affairs of the EAC is recognised through various articles of the EACT. Article 7 describes civil society as one of the crucial actors in the EAC. Article 127 envisages the creation of an enabling environment for both civil society and the private sector to participate in the affairs of the Community. The article specifically demands the promotion of the roles of non-governmental organisations (NGOs). The quest for participation of civil society is underpinned by the realisation that the initial Community (EAC 1) failed partly as a result of non-involvement of citizens in its activities. Even so, the initial design of the process did not take into consideration the involvement of CSOs until after CSOs intervened through the Non-Governmental Organisations Coalition for East Africa. It is out of this intervention that some consensus was reached allowing civil society participation in the affairs of the Community. Table 2.11 shows how the EACT provides for civil society participation.

Table 2.11 Provision by the EACT for civil society participation in the EAC

Article	Provision
5.3(g)	"the Community will ensure, inter alia, the enhancement and strengthening of partnerships with civil society, so as to achieve sustainable socio-economic and political development"
127.1	"the partner states agree to provide an enabling environment for the participation of civil society in the development activities within the Community"
127.3	"the partner states undertake to promote a continuous dialogue with civil society at both the national and the Community level"
127.4	"the Secretary-General shall provide the forum for consultations between civil society organisations, the private sector, other interest groups and appropriate institutions of the Community"

Source: EACT

The EAC established a Department of Gender, Community Development and Civil Society to be the liaison with CSOs. The department works under the Directorate of Social Sectors, one of the eight directorates in the EAC. It also falls directly under the Deputy Secretary-General for Productive and Social Services, who in turn reports to the Secretary-General.

As the focal point for civil society, the department has suffered from lack of capacity to handle the many requests for civil society participation in the EAC. All accounts indicate that the one person handling all civil society matters in the department is overwhelmed and unless the department is capacitated, civil society participation will continue to be hampered. This aspect is made even more significant by the overly restrictive rules for granting observer status.

2.7.2 Observer status at the EAC

In order to facilitate civil society participation in the EAC, Rules of Granting Observer Status at the EAC were formulated in 2001. "Observers" can be foreign countries, intergovernmental organisations or CSOs. "Observer status" is the entitlement conferred upon these entities to send observers on invitation to the meetings of the organs of the Community.

Of concern to CSOs are the broad and specific criteria for their admission. The broad criteria are:

- Acceptance of the fundamental principles underlying the EAC;
- Interest in the fundamental and operational principles of the EAC;
- Contribution towards the strengthening of regional integration in East Africa; and
- Ability to enhance development partnership.

The specific criteria are:

- The organisation should have objectives of common interest to the partner states;
- The organisation's activities should have a regional dimension, with the organisation being registered in each of the partner states; and
- In its regional activities, the organisation should have a track record of at least three years of active operation.

Article 5 of the Rules provides the procedures for actual participation by observers. Two overarching conditions that are of interest to CSOs are:

- Presence at official openings and closings of all meetings of the Community; and
- Attendance of meetings of the organs of the Community dealing with subjects of interest to observers.

The specific conditions for participation are as follows:

- Observers may, with the express authority of the chairperson, participate in the proceedings of the meeting to which they are invited.
- Observers may, at the request of the chairperson of a meeting, make a statement on a matter of particular interest to them, provided that the text of the statement is presented to the chairperson through the Secretary-General before it is made.
- The chairperson of the meeting may give the observers an opportunity to reply to questions which may be directly addressed to them in a meeting.
- Observers do not have the right to vote.

The Rules have been criticised for being restrictive and not facilitating civil society participation in the affairs of the Community. For example, the two requirements that an organisation's activities should have a regional dimension, with the organisation being registered in each of the partner states, and that the organisation must have a track record of regional activities for the past three years, are particularly limiting. Mere registration of an organisation in all the partner states neither increases its ability to participate nor the relevance of its agenda to the EAC. Likewise, longevity of existence does not guarantee the relevance of the agenda of the organisation.

So far, 15 organisations have been granted observer status:

- East African Business Council (EABC);
- East African Local Government Association;
- East African National Networks of Aids Service Organisations (EANNASO);
- East African Support Unit for NGOs;

- Society for International Development – Office for East Africa;

- East African Trade Union Congress;

- Southern and Eastern African Trade Information and Negotiations Institute;

- Association of Professional Societies in East Africa;

- Africa Women's Economic Policy Network;

- East African Communities' Organization for Management of Lake Victoria Resources;

- East African Centre for Constitutional Development Forum (Kituo cha Katiba);

- East African Human Rights Institute;

- East Africa Law Society (EALS); and

- East African Magistrates and Judges Association.

The shortcomings of the Rules have led to a number of other approaches by civil society. Some organisations have opted to form alternative platforms of engagement. Alternative platforms of this nature include EACSOF and the various platforms created through the support of Trade Mark East Africa (Table 2.12).

Table 2.12 The various platforms and their host institutions

Platform	Host organisation	When formed
East Africa Health Platform	East African Business Council	2012
Women and Business Platform	East African Business Council	2012
Governance and Human Rights Platform	EALS	2012

East African Civil Society Organisations' Forum

The process of putting together an alternative engagement platform started in 2008 and was informed mainly by the restrictive nature of the Rules of Granting Observer Status.

EACSOF was formed in 2008. However, before the formation of EACSOF, there were attempts to form a consultative structure for CSOs. For example, the EAC Secretariat hosted the first regional workshop for CSOs between 28 and 29 July 2005 with the theme "Civil Society Mobilisation for Effective Participation in the EAC".

The initial efforts culminated in a raft of recommendations toward formation of the EAC NGO/CSO Steering Committee, an Economic and Social Committee, an EAC NGO/CSO Forum, a secretariat to coordinate the affairs of the Forum and a People's Forum. Further proposals were an annual meeting of CSOs as part of the EAC Calendar of Activities and the introduction of consultative status for CSOs, "which do not have to be subjected to the requirements of the observer status criteria".

These efforts did not bear much fruit and therefore civil society under the auspices of the EALS started the process of putting together EACSOF as a civil society-driven platform. The EALS also provided hosting for EACSOF before it became an independent institution from 2012. The organisation, which is based in Arusha, is led by a Governing Council made up of 15 members (these have now been reduced to ten). The Governing Council is elected by the members in annual general meetings that take place once every year. EACSOF has membership from all five partner states.

EACSOF is embedded in the EAC Consultative Dialogue Framework for Civil Society and Private Sector as the contact organisation for civil society. Consequently, even though it still does not have observer status with the EAC, it has received invitations to many of the meetings of the EAC. One of its most enduring activities has been the Annual Governance Conferences which it undertakes together with the EAC Secretariat. The Governance Conferences are undertaken in order to inform the key debates in the region. After every Governance Conference, a communiqué is issued. EACSOF also issues communiqués after every annual general meeting.

2.7.3 Memoranda of understanding

In order to be effective in their advocacy work at the EAC, some organisations have opted to have more direct relationships with the EAC by, for instance, negotiating and signing MoUs with the Secretariat. MoUs have enabled civil society to engage with the EAC. Some of the areas of engagement are:

- Formulation of the East African HIV and AIDS Prevention and Management Bill led by EANNASO;

- Formulation of the Gender Protocol led by EASSI;

- Formulation of the East African Human Rights Bill led by Kituo Cha Katiba;

- Formulation of the Consultative Dialogue Framework for Civil Society and Private;

- Sector Participation in the EAC Integration Process; and

- Engagement in cross-border activities.

Eastern African Subregional Support Initiative for the Advancement of Women (EASSI)

The MoU between EASSI and the EAC was signed in 2010. The organisation was then leading the East Africa Declaration on Gender Equality Campaign towards the adoption of an EAC gender Protocol. The MoU is based on the requirement on the part of the EAC to foster cooperation arrangements with various interest groups including civil society. Further, the EACT also recognises the contribution of women towards socio-economic transformation and sustainable growth.

2.7.4 The EAC CSO mobilisation strategy

The EAC developed a draft CSO Mobilisation Strategy in line with Article 127(4), aimed at creating a framework for structured dialogue. It is hoped that inputs from civil society will be appropriately channelled to the EAC and the partner states. The strategy recognises the need to mobilise civil society for more effective participation. Through the strategy, the EAC commits to partner with civil society in capacity-building and support programmes. It seeks to involve the private sector to partner with civil society and enhance civil society's voice in engaging with the EAC. Even though the Strategy was developed by a consultant, civil society played an important role, with the facilitation of EACSOF.

According to the strategy, specific areas of capacity-building for civil society are:

- Policy formulation and analysis;

- Policy negotiation and identification; and

- Packaging and distribution of high development impact information and materials to citizens at all levels of orientation.

In concrete terms, the strategy identifies avenues for mobilisation. These include the following:

- Development and operationalisation of an Institutionalised Dialogue Framework;

- Scaling up supply of information and awareness on the EAC and its processes;

- Enhancing an open-door policy in partner states and public–private dialogue;

- Mapping out relevant CSOs;

- Strengthening EACSOF, its operations, representatives and effectiveness;

- Promoting collaboration and building of networks amongst CSOs; and

- Developing and strengthening partnerships with the EAC Secretariat, partner states, the private sector and other interest groups.

The mobilisation framework presents a critical entry point for collaboration between CSOs and the EAC. In and of itself, it creates an aura of a positive and mutually beneficial relationship between the two. It also feeds into other relationships that have been established, for example, by individual organisations such as EASSI and by networks such as EACSOF. The added value is that of structuring participation.

2.7.5 The Consultative Dialogue Framework

One of the key priorities set out by the CSOs Mobilisation Strategy was completion of the EAC Consultative Dialogue Framework for Civil Society and Private Sector Participation in the EAC Integration Process. Its development was undertaken by a consultant supported by the Deutsche Gesellschaft für Internationale Zusammenarbeit and the EAC Secretariat. The Secretariat had identified it as a priority.

The framework, which is in line with Article 127 of the EACT, recognises the EABC as the focal point for the private sector and EACSOF as the focal point for civil society. However, the structure is dynamic enough to accommodate other interests. It envisages formal and informal processes. Continuous dialogue will take place between the EAC, partner states, CSOs, public service organisations and other interest groups, both at the national and regional level. National dialogue will be coordinated through the ministries responsible for EAC affairs. Regional dialogue will take place in accordance with the EAC Calendar of Activities and an Annual Forum will be convened by the Secretary-General. Figure 2.4 is a diagrammatic presentation of the Consultative Dialogue Framework.

It also provides for the following rules of procedure to govern the dialogue process:

- An agenda for the meeting should be developed by a dialogue committee composed of representatives from the EAC Secretariat, CSOs, PSOs and other interest groups.

- The Community should set aside basic resources to cover the meeting expenses for the Annual Forum, while parties to the dialogue should contribute to the dialogue process by being responsible for their travel-related expenses.

- The composition of participants to the annual forum should adhere to the need for equal representation between private sector and civil society and regional representations from partner states. It should also provide representation for other interest groups.

- The Chairperson of the Summit or of the Council of Ministers or their designate should grace either the opening or closing session of the Secretary-General's Forum. The Speaker of EALA and the Judge President of the EACJ or their representatives should also be invited to grace the forum.

- As far as possible, decisions arising from the Secretary-General's Forum should be taken by consensus.

- Decisions and/or recommendations should be prepared in any of the following formats or a combination of them: policy briefs, advices, communiqués, position papers, summarised research reports and agenda or inputs and should be forwarded to the relevant organs of the EAC for their further action.

- The Secretary-General should lay before the Council the policy recommendations coming out of the Annual Secretary-General's Forum for further action by the Council.

- The decision of the Council on the recommendations tabled before it should be formally circulated to the members but also formally tabled at the next Secretary-General's forum for notification and further action.

In 2012, the Secretary-General's Forum was held in Nairobi. Its theme was: "The EAC We Want: Focusing on the Quick Wins". EACSOF played a significant role in convening the Forum.

Figure 2.4 A diagrammatic representation of the Consultative Dialogue Framework

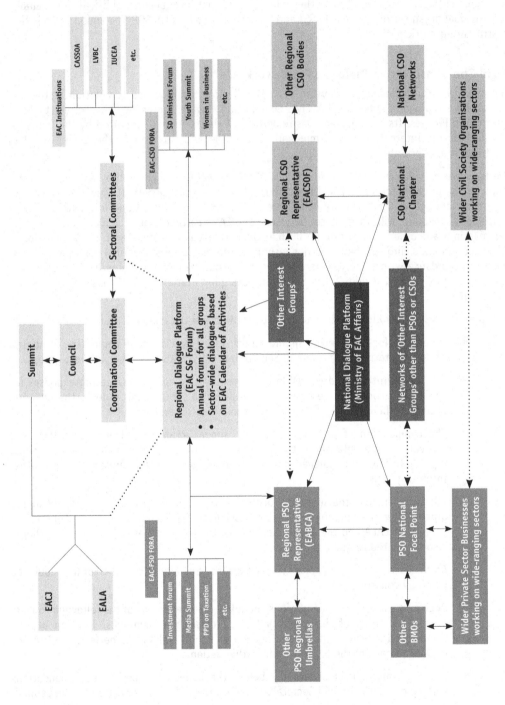

2.8 Current debates in the EAC

The integration of East Africa was envisaged, in Article 5(2) of the EACT, to be a linear process involving the following steps:

1. The Customs Union;

2. The Common Market;

3. The Monetary Union; and

4. Political Federation.

Many current debates within the EAC focus on subsequent processes, while some focus on the challenges that continue to face the process. This section discusses some of these debates.

2.8.1 The emerging peace and security architecture in the EAC

Conflict has been a key challenge in the Horn of Africa and the Great Lakes region. It has been stated already that the EAC partner states work largely through IGAD on peace and security. This is partly because IGAD has developed a more elaborate peace and security infrastructure compared with that of the EAC. IGAD also has a longer history of engaging with the AU on issues of peace and security.

With the adoption of the Peace and Security Protocol in the meeting of the Summit in February 2013, the EAC is on track to develop its own peace and security infrastructure even though this will still be pegged on the AU infrastructure, mainly through the African Peace and Security Architecture (APSA). At the end of 2013, the Protocol had not been ratified by all EAC partner states. However, the adoption of the Protocol signified an intention to focus more seriously on security. It must be emphasised that the peace and security infrastructure is just emerging and the EAC does not yet have the capacity to deploy troops.

In essence, APSA is a mechanism that enables the AU, RECs and Regional Mechanisms for Conflict Prevention, Management and Resolution, to engage in peace and security in line with the AU Protocol establishing the Peace and Security Council. To this end, RECs – including the EAC – are in the process of establishing standby forces.

2.8.2 The emerging two-speed integration process

It has already been mentioned that decision-making at the EAC is by consensus. This gives a veto power to all partner states on particular decisions. However, it does not mean that other partner states do not have the power to proceed on issues of mutual interest. The principle of variable geometry provided for in the EACT allows for progression in cooperation among a sub-group of members in a larger integration scheme in a variety of areas and at different speeds; this enables partner states to adopt different "speeds" in the integration process.

Kenya, Rwanda and Uganda have applied the principle on several occasions to make and implement decisions that did not seem agreeable to Tanzania and Burundi. Of note were two meetings that took place in 2013, one in Entebbe and another in Mombasa. The first "Trilateral Summit on Regional Infrastructure, Trade and Political and Economic Integration" took place in June 2013 and ended up with assignments for each of the leaders/countries. It was decided that Kenya would take a lead in pipeline and electricity generation and distribution; Rwanda would take on Customs, a single visa and the EAC e-identity card; and Uganda would lead in railways and political federation.

The second meeting in Mombasa saw the launch of Berth 19 at the Mombasa Port, as one of the steps towards upgrading the port to meet the challenges experienced in movement of goods across the region.

Tanzania's reaction to the trilateral meetings and agreements between Kenya, Rwanda and Uganda was to claim that the country was being sidelined in the integration process and that the decisions being made were illegal. This demonstrated the sensitivity of the trilateral initiative. The key lesson from this is that whereas the Treaty provides for variable geometry, the politics of integration complicates its application.

2.8.3 Tanzania's "defensiveness" in engaging with the EAC

Some observers of Tanzania's recent engagements with the EAC have criticised the country for lack of commitment to the integration process. Terming the country's engagement as "timid defensiveness", analysts Ahmed Salim and Aidan Eyakuze in a 2012 essay are categorical that the country and its leadership are no longer supporting the integration process. This is how they put it in their report: "Tanzania is unenthusiastic about the EAC regional integration project and is the main reason why the process is so slow." The writers call upon Tanzania to decide whether it is in or out of the integration process. They argue that fence-sitting will hurt the people of Tanzania.

In discussing the emerging "two-speed" integration process, in which Kenya, Uganda and Rwanda decided to apply the principle of variable geometry, they state that the three countries have proceeded to make important decisions that bind them to move the integration process forward and that the embrace of variable geometry is an indication of lack of cohesion and common understanding among the key decision-makers in the EAC.

In four "exhibits", the writers give concrete examples of incidents attributed to Tanzania that support their conclusions:

- The temporary closure of the Taveta border crossing point (between Tanzania and Kenya) in February 2012, which resulted from Kenyan traders complaining about the imposition of a USD 200 fee on motorists from Kenya.

- Tanzania's ban on non-governmental exports of maize and grain for six months while Kenya was facing famine. Kenya retaliated by imposing a ban on the export of seeds from some parts of the Western and Rift Valley provinces of Kenya.

- Tanzania's reluctance to sign up to the establishment of the EAC Political Federation and the Common Defence Pact.

- A Tanzanian High Court ruling against the EADB. The financial implications of the ruling could have bankrupted the bank, had a political solution not been found.

After analysing these exhibits, Salim and Eyakuze opined that Tanzania should move from timid defensiveness to confident engagement on the basis of certain assets that the country possesses:

- *Political capital*: Tanzania has an impressive history of mediating conflict in the region.

- *Demography and geography*: It is the largest and most populous of the EAC nations.

- *Resources*: Tanzania is unmatched in the region, for example, in energy and land resources.

2.8.4 The COMESA–EAC–SADC tripartite engagement

The envisaged construction of the African Economic Community in line with the Abuja Treaty requires the strengthening of RECs as the building blocks of the continental union. The AU recognises eight RECs across the regions of Africa as its building blocks in this scheme.

The three RECs with overlapping membership (COMESA, EAC and SADC) commenced tripartite discussions to form one regional bloc. It is envisaged that the three will form a Free Trade Area (FTA) and subsequently a Customs Union. The resultant trade area will encompass 28 countries with a population of 527 million and a GDP of USD 624 billion. Apart from quickening the process of continental integration, this will also deal with the problem of overlapping membership.

The declaration launching the negotiations for the establishment of the FTA was signed during the second COMESA–EAC–SADC Tripartite Summit of Heads of State and Government held in Johannesburg, South Africa, on 12 June 2011. The Tripartite Trade Negotiation Forum is the institution charged with the negotiations.

This is an important debate in the integration initiative with which civil society ought to engage, since the ultimate goal for the continent is to achieve full integration. The civil society networks working in specific RECs should work together to influence the continental integration effort.

2.8.5 Expanding the membership of the EAC

The EAC restarted in 1999 with three member states – Kenya, Tanzania and Uganda. In 2007, Rwanda and Burundi joined. Since then, both Sudan and South Sudan (which became independent from Sudan in 2011) have applied to join the Community. In 2011, the Summit turned down Sudan's application on the basis that it did not meet the criteria of geographical proximity and adherence to universal standards of human rights. The decision seems to have taken account of the criticisms levelled against Sudan for human rights violations, particularly in the Darfur region. However, Sudan and the partner states of the EAC are also members of COMESA.

In February 2012, Somalia also made an application to join the Community. A decision on this is still pending.

Expansion of the membership of the EAC ought to take into account the need to consolidate the Community given the level it has reached. The complexities of integration are such that any new member who joins an integration process is likely to come in with a raft of issues that require resolution and that may cause a level of discomfort. They also come into a process that is already in motion. A careful evaluation of the pros and cons of inviting new members and their worth to the process must be undertaken.

2.8.6 Rising poverty levels within a situation of deepening integration

The Society for International Development in its 2012 report *The State of East Africa* highlighted the contradiction that whereas business between the partner states is booming, the people of East Africa are becoming poorer and poorer. The report noted the expansion of trade between the partner states, from USD 2.2 billion in 2005 to USD 4.1 billion in 2010. However, at the same time, it pointed out, "data suggests the number of East Africans living below the poverty line increased from 44 million to 53 million, even though all countries, with the exception of Burundi and Kenya, reduced the share of their population who lived below the respective national poverty line." Even though partner states' economies grew faster than the rate of population growth, "the distribution of the expanding wealth has not been equitable."

To the extent that the Treaty envisages a people-driven Community, civil society needs to raise questions about these trends. If integration does not end in the advancement of the welfare of the people, then the EAC shall find itself constantly confronting challenges of legitimacy.

2.8.7 Challenges in implementation of the Customs Union

Implementation of the Customs Union started in 2005 with the coming into force of the Protocol Establishing the Customs Union on 1 January 2005. The Customs Union had the following objectives:

- Further liberalisation of intraregional trade in goods, on the basis of mutually beneficial trade agreements among the partner states;
- Promotion of efficiency in production within the Community;
- Enhancement of domestic, cross-border and foreign investment in the Community; and
- Promotion of economic development and diversification in industrialisation in the Community.

To further facilitate implementation of the Customs Union, a number of annexures were formulated. These include:

- East African Rules of Origin;
- List of Goods Restricted and Prohibited from Trade; and
- East African Community Customs Union (Freeport Operations) Regulations.

Some of the key steps taken to facilitate the operations of the Customs Union are:

- Harmonisation of macro-economic policies;
- Liberalisation of interest rates and exchange rate regimes;
- Harmonisation of investment incentives and fiscal policies; and
- Putting in place double taxation regimes.

However, the implementation of the Customs Union did not go smoothly and controversy and challenges abound.

The removal of non-tariff barriers (NTBs), for instance, continues to be a major issue of controversy. In June 2007, member states put in place committees to monitor removal of NTBs. The problem of incomplete removal of NTBs remains a thorny issue in the integration process and one of the ongoing debates. Some notable NTBs are:

- Customs and administrative documentation procedures;
- Immigration procedures;
- Cumbersome inspection requirements;
- Police roadblocks;
- Varying trade regulations among EAC countries; and
- Varying, cumbersome and costly transiting procedures in the EAC countries.

2.8.8 Challenges in implementation of the Common Market

The EAC entered the Common Market phase on 1 July 2010 after five years of implementation of the Customs Union, even though some of the controversies in the implementation of the Customs Union were yet to be resolved. The Protocol on the Establishment of the East African Common Market provides the road map towards realising an integrated market with a population of almost 150 million citizens. The broad objective of the Common Market, according to Article 4 of the Protocol, is to widen and deepen cooperation among the partner states in the economic and social fields for the benefit of the partner states.

During negotiations on the Common Market Protocol, for instance, the question of land proved to be divisive. The Tanzanian government felt strongly that land should not be a matter for EAC discussion. Indeed, the Common Market Protocol in Article 15 states that "The partner states hereby agree that access to and use of land and premises shall be governed by the national policies and laws of the partner states."

This initial disagreement was followed by disagreements over provisions involving free movement of labour. This is reflected in the issue of work permits. Even though the Protocol provides that "partner states undertake to harmonise their labour policies, national laws and programmes to facilitate the free movement of labour within the Community", implementation proves to be a Herculean task.

If the intention of the partner states was to work towards free movement of labour, then this intention was quickly betrayed by the actions of the partner states. Whereas Rwanda soon allowed East African citizens free access to work in the country without the requirement of work permits,

Tanzania increased foreign work permit fees, arguing that it was an important source of revenue – the cost was raised by 33%. In August 2012, Tanzania raised fees for workers engaged in prospecting and mining. It also increased the fees for large-scale traders and businessmen, who were required to pay USD 3,000, almost double the previous USD 1,600. Tanzania also argued that the East African region had not reached the level of integration that necessitates abolition of work permits.

Partner states are yet to cede sovereignty to EAC institutions, which is key to managing national interests in a way which will ensure that trade benefits all members. Resistance to implementation of certain aspects of protocols reveals a nationalist posturing by the partner states, looking at issues through a national rather than collective interest prism.

Advances in trade could also be undermined by external interests. Global powers are stepping up the scramble for the region – in 2011 China signed a Trade and Investment Framework Agreement (TIFA) with the EAC that will focus on the promotion of commodity trade, tourism, investment, infrastructure development and human resource training. The USA and the EAC are in the process of crafting a new investment treaty for the EAC to replace the 2008 TIFA.

The EAC and the EU have been in talks since 2007 over a new economic partnership agreement. Countries are concerned that several analyses have shown that economic partnership agreements will have negative effects on their economies, including

- A stifling loss of critical tariff revenues;
- Deepened de-industrialisation;
- Suffocation of small and medium-scale enterprises;
- Collapse of the agricultural sector;
- Exacerbated unemployment;
- Increased poverty levels; and
- Regional disintegration.

The negotiations present a real test to EAC common positions. Only time will tell if the agreement will be signed between the EAC and the EU or whether some EAC members will opt out and enter into bilateral agreements with the EU.

Given the power imbalance between the EAC and the external actors mentioned above, there is a need for mechanisms to ensure citizens' input into ongoing and future negotiations on trade to safeguard citizens' interests. More engagement by non-state actors in this area is crucial to ensure that trade pacts with external partners promote regional integration priorities, especially poverty reduction and job creation.

2.8.9 Funding for the EAC and the issue of self-reliance

The EAC is funded by partner states as well as development partners (see Table 2.8). The 2012/2013 budget factored in a contribution of just over 29% (contributions through ministries in charge of EAC affairs and through "other agencies") from partner states. The contribution expected from donors was the largest, amounting to more than 70%. The expected donor contribution was therefore more than double the contribution by partner states.

The donor funding regime has been criticised for not impacting on the lives of the citizens of East Africa. Such funding often went into facilitating workshops, travel and consultancies. Such funds therefore eventually found their way back to the same donors since they also contracted consultants for the many studies undertaken and workshops facilitated.

Bibliography and resources

Adar, KG & Centre for Studies on Federalism (2011) *The Democratisation of International Organisations: The East African Community*. http://www.internationaldemocracywatch.org/ attachments/458_EAC-adar.pdf, accessed 4 September 2012

AFRIMAP, AFRODAD & OXFAM (2007) *Towards a People-Driven African Union: Current Obstacles and New Opportunities*

Deya, D (2007) Constitutionalism and the East African Community in 2004. In: L Mute (ed.) *Constitutionalism in East Africa: Progress, Challenges and Prospects in 2004*. Fountain Publishers Ltd

Dijk, T (no date) *Background Paper, Civil Society Participation within the East African Community*

Gathii, J *Mission Creep or a Search for Relevance: The East African Court of Justice's Human Rights Strategy*. pp. 24–25. http://ssrn.com/abstract=2178756

Kituo Cha Katiba, *A Draft Bill of Rights for the East African Community*

Odhiambo, M (2010) *Towards Greater Civil Society Participation in the East African Community: Challenges and Prospects*. Kituo Cha Katiba Occasional Publication 5, Fountain Publishers, Kampala

Odhiambo, M (ed.) (2012) *Annual State of Constitutionalism in East Africa 2010*. Kituo Cha Katiba

Oloo, A *The East African Legislative Assembly: Which Way Forward?* (Mimeo)

SID (2012) *The State of East Africa 2012*

Legal notices

Legal Notice No. EAC/11/2007. http://www.eac.int/customs/index.php?option=com_ docman&Itemid=123 accessed 28/09/2012

The Protocol on Relations between the African Union and the RECs. http://www.afrimap.org/ english/images/treaty/AU-RECs-Protocol.pdf accessed 25/08/2012

Cases

East Africa Law Society & 4 Others vs. the Attorney-General of Kenya & 3 Others, Reference No. 3 of 2010

Katabazi and 21 Others vs. Secretary-General of the East African Community and Another (Ref. No. 1 of 2007) [2007] EACJ 3 (1 November 2007)

Prof. Peter Anyang Nyong'o and 10 Others vs. The Attorney-General of Kenya and 5 Others

Reports

EAC Budget Speech, 2012

EAC, *An Evaluation of the Implementation and Impact of the East African Community Customs Union*, 2009 http://www.google.co.ke/#hl=sw&site=&source=hp&q=An+Evaluation+of+the+Implementat ion+and+Impact+of+the+East+African+Community+Customs+Union%2C+2009+&oq

EAC, First Workshop for Civil Society in East Africa, AICC, Arusha, Tanzania, 28– 29 July 2005, Workshop Recommendations, Ref. EAC/01/CSO/2005

EAC, Report of the Committee on Fast Tracking East African Federation, Submitted to the Sixth Summit of Heads of State of the East African Community, Arusha, Tanzania, 26 November 2004

EAC, Report of the Legal and Policy Audit and Emerging Issues for Inclusion in the Proposed East African Law on HIV/AIDS, African Vision Integrated Strategies (IS) Consultants

EAC, The East African Court of Justice, 10th Year Report, November 2011

Pan-African Lawyers Union (PALU), Report of the Roundtable Discussion on EACJ appeal No. 1 of 2011 (IMLU Case) and on the Draft Protocol on Extending the Jurisdiction of the EACJ

EAC contacts

EAC Liaison Office at the AU

Head: Mr Joseph Birungi
+251 913 545171
tirumanywam@africa-union.org

AU Headquarters
Building C, Ground Floor, Roosevelt Street (Old Airport Area) / PO Box 3243
W12 K19, Addis Ababa, Ethiopia

AU Liaison Office to the EAC

Head: Mr Ben Balthazar Rutsinga
+255 758 532114
rutsingab@africa-union.org

EAC Headquarters
EAC Close, off Africa Mashariki Road / PO Box 1096
Arusha, Tanzania

Gender, Youth and Community Development Department

Contact person: Mrs Generose Minani
+255 27 2162100
gminani@eachq.org

EAC Headquarters
EAC Close, off Afrika Mashariki Road / PO Box 1096
Arusha, Tanzania

3. The Economic Community of West African States

Abbreviations and acronyms

AEC	African Economic Community
APSA	Peace and Security Architecture
AU	African Union's
CDD	Centre for Democracy and Development
CEAO	*Communauté Economique des Etats de l'Afrique de l'Ouest*
CET	Common External Tariff
EBID	ECOWAS Bank for Investment and Development
ECCJ	ECOWAS Community Court of Justice
ECHP	ECOWAS Common Humanitarian Policy
ECONEC	ECOWAS Network of Electoral Commissions
ECOWARN	ECOWAS–WANEP collaborative framework
ECOWAS	Economic Community of West African States
ECPF	ECOWAS Conflict Prevention Framework
EU	European Union
EUR	euro
FARE	Forum of Associations Recognised by ECOWAS
FCFA	West African CFA franc
GIABA	Intergovernmental Action Group against Money Laundering in West Africa
MFWA	Media Foundation for West Africa
MoU	memorandum of understanding
MSC	Mediation and Security Council
OSIWA	Open Society Initiative for West Africa
SERAP	Socio-Economic Rights and Accountability Project
UEMOA	*Union Monétaire et Economique Ouest Africaine* (West African Economic and Monetary Union)
WABA	West African Bar Association
WACSOF	West African Civil Society Forum
WAHO	West African Health Organisation
WANEP	West African Network for Peace-building

3.1 Historical background and legal framework

3.1.1 Historical background of ECOWAS

The Economic Community of West African States (ECOWAS) sits on the Gulf of Benin between the Sahara Desert and the Gulf of Guinea and occupies an area of about 5.1 million km[2] (17% of the total area of Africa) with a population of approximately 300 million. The subregion is bounded on the north by Algeria, Libya and Chad, on the west by Mauritania, on the south by the Gulf of Guinea and on the east by Cameroon. With an annual budget of USD 600 million, ECOWAS is arguably the most prominent integration scheme in the West African region. After the failure of initial attempts at integration immediately following independence, cooperation arrangements based on colonial groupings began with limited success. This trend was especially evident in francophone West Africa as states previously colonised by France achieved a measure of success in their bid to integrate socio-economically.

Although ECOWAS is a post-colonial initiative, some commentators trace military and socio-economic cooperation between the peoples of the West African region back to the 19th century. During the colonial period itself, the seeds of integration in West Africa were further nurtured, especially in the parts of the region that came under French colonial rule. The most obvious evidence of this was the creation of French West Africa by French colonial authorities in 1895. Ghana and Guinea created the Union of West African States in November 1958 in Accra, while in 1961, Cote d'Ivoire, Haute-Volta, Dahomey and Niger created the Conseil de l'Entente.

The more recent history of collective integration in West Africa dates back to the early 1960s. By popular account, the foundation for the establishment of modern-day ECOWAS was laid by President William Tubman of Liberia. The actualisation of President Tubman's idea of a free trade area in West Africa took the form of an agreement between Cote d'Ivoire, Guinea, Liberia and Sierra Leone that was signed in February 1965. However, not much came out of that agreement, as its envisaged outcome, the "Organisation for West African Cooperation" did not materialise, as a result of the unpreparedness of the countries involved. Notwithstanding the demise of President Tubman's initiative, efforts at integration continued in the region, mostly along colonial–linguistic lines.

In the Francophone zone, the Union Douanière de l'Afrique de l'Ouest,[1] created in June 1959 in Paris to promote free movement of goods and a single tariff for imported goods, was replaced in January 1966 by the Union Douanière des Etats de l'Afrique de l'Ouest,[2] a more structured institution[3] aimed at introducing a common external tariff scheme for original products of the region. In June 1972, a treaty establishing the Communauté Economique des Etats de l'Afrique de l'Ouest (CEAO) was signed in Bamako, Mali, by the same countries to "promote harmonised and balanced development of member states' economies in order to improve the living standards of their citizens".[4] In 1994, CEAO was transformed into the Union Monétaire et Economique Ouest Africaine (West African Economic and Monetary Union) (UEMOA).

In the anglophone area, Sierra Leone and Liberia formed in 1974 the Mano River Union and were joined by Guinea some years later.

In April 1972, General Yakubu Gowon, the military head of state of Nigeria, and General Gnassingbé Eyadéma, the military head of state of Togo, jointly revived the idea of regional integration, and began consultations in that regard. These two military leaders prompted the drafting of the framework for a new regional organisation and began to solicit the support of other heads of state in the region. By December 1973, Generals Gowon and Eyadéma were able to bring together stakeholders to consider a first framework document in Lomé, Togo. This was closely followed in early 1974 by a meeting of experts and jurists in Accra, Ghana, and a meeting of ministers in Monrovia, Liberia, in January 1975.

---

1   It included Cote d'Ivoire, Dahomey (Benin), Upper Volta (Burkina Faso), Mauritania, Niger and the Federation of Mali (Mali and Senegal).

2   The membership included Cote d'Ivoire, Upper Volta (Burkina Faso), Mali, Mauritania, Niger and Senegal.

3   With a Secretary General, a Committee of Experts and a Council of Ministers.

4   See Article 3 of the Treaty establishing ECOWAS.

The 1975 Treaty

On 28 May 1975, representatives of 15 countries converged on Lagos, Nigeria, to sign the ECOWAS Treaty, which also became known as the Treaty of Lagos. The 15 countries that signed the 1975 ECOWAS Treaty were: Benin, Burkina Faso (then known as Upper Volta), Cote d'Ivoire, The Gambia, Ghana, Guinea, Guinea-Bissau, Liberia, Mali, Mauritania, Niger, Nigeria, Senegal, Sierra Leone and Togo. Most of these states ratified the 1975 ECOWAS Treaty between June and July 1975. Guinea-Bissau and Mauritania ratified the instrument in March 1976. In 1977, Cape Verde became the 16th member of ECOWAS when it ratified and acceded to the 1975 ECOWAS Treaty. There is insufficient material to analyse civil society involvement and input in the evolution of ECOWAS at this stage.

Since its establishment was prompted by the need to forge a collective response to post-independence economic challenges, ECOWAS was founded as a vehicle for economic integration. The organisation was expected to provide a platform for member states to pursue the "accelerated and sustained economic development of their states" that would lead to the unity of the countries of West Africa. Accordingly, the objectives of ECOWAS were to promote cooperation and development in all fields of economic activity for the purpose of raising the standard of living of West African peoples, increase and maintain economic stability, foster closer relations among member states and contribute to the progress and development of the African continent. In addition to these economic objectives, it was understood by the founding fathers that ECOWAS was also supposed to provide a platform "to give the member states a stronger voice in African affairs and in international affairs".

The 1993 Revised Treaty

By the late 1980s, the popular conclusion was that the lofty objectives of ECOWAS were not being realised. A series of unfortunate events, notable among which were the internal conflicts in Sierra Leone and Liberia, ensured that ECOWAS got sucked into the internal politics and security of its member states. The most extreme form of its intervention was the deployment of ECOWAS-sponsored military forces in conflict-ridden member states either for peacekeeping or to monitor ECOWAS-initiated or -supported ceasefire agreements. These military interventions took place despite the fact that the 1975 ECOWAS Treaty did not envisage any political or security role for the organisation. The consciousness that the Community was moving beyond its strict economic mandate led the ECOWAS Heads of State and Government to set up a high-profile Committee of Eminent Persons to re-examine the foundations of ECOWAS, bearing in mind the dynamics of a changing society. The report of the Committee of Eminent Persons provided the immediate impetus for the revision of the 1975 ECOWAS Treaty. The result was the drafting and subsequent adoption of a revised ECOWAS Treaty by the Heads of State and Government of member states. The ECOWAS Revised Treaty was signed in Cotonou, Benin, on 24 July 1993.

Between July 1993 and August 1997, 14 states ratified the revised Treaty, resulting in its entry into force on 23 August 1995. As at December 2011, Guinea-Bissau was the only state that had not ratified the revised ECOWAS Treaty, even though it continues to participate actively in the processes and activities of the Community. Six years after the signing of the revised Treaty, membership of ECOWAS was again reduced to 15 with the withdrawal of Mauritania in December 1999. The current member states are: Benin, Burkina Faso, Cape Verde, Cote d'Ivoire, Gambia, Ghana, Guinea, Guinea Bissau, Liberia, Mali, Niger, Nigeria, Senegal, Sierra Leone and Togo.

In view of the difficulties experienced under the 1975 Treaty, the revision process targeted critical improvements in the ECOWAS Treaty framework. The highlights of the 1993 revision include the expansion of the ECOWAS objectives to provide for the establishment of an economic union, as well as a monetary union, and the expansion of areas of ECOWAS competence. The level of civil society involvement in the process, if any, was barely documented and is therefore difficult to gauge. However, the impact that these socio-economic activities have on the daily lives of the people of West Africa requires greater involvement of civil society in the shaping of ECOWAS policies in these areas.

For the first time, the revised Treaty outlined fundamental principles to guide the integration agenda and processes. The principles in the revised Treaty include:

- Non-aggression among ECOWAS states;

- Maintenance of regional peace, stability and security;

- Peaceful settlement of disputes;

- Recognition, promotion and protection of human rights in accordance with the African Charter on Human and Peoples' Rights; and

- Promotion and consolidation of a democratic system of governance in member states.

It is noteworthy that the question of peace, security and stability of member states, which was not included in the 1975 Treaty, features prominently in the 1993 revised Treaty. The expanded fundamental principles created greater room for civil society involvement in ECOWAS business.

Other improvements in the revised Treaty included the expansion of the General Undertakings to include an obligation on the part of member states to "honour ... obligations under this Treaty and to abide by the decisions and regulations of the Community", and to take action in accordance with their national constitutions to give internal legal force to the implementation of Community laws. The revised Treaty also introduced additional Community institutions:

- Community Parliament;

- Economic and Social Council;

- Community Court of Justice (a transformation from Tribunal under the earlier Treaty); and

- Fund for Cooperation, Compensation and Development.

The creation of additional institutions that are closer to the ordinary citizen was intended to be a catalyst for enhanced civil society engagement with the Community.

The revised Treaty further added areas of cooperation that exceeded the narrow economic focus of the 1975 Treaty. Thus, for instance, Chapter X of the 1993 revised Treaty provides for "Cooperation in Political, Judicial and Legal Affairs, Regional Security and Immigration". Chapter X also includes Article 56, which contains an agreement to cooperate on political matters, including cooperation for the purpose of realising the objectives of instruments such as the African Charter on Human and Peoples' Rights (African Charter). Significantly, in Article 58, ECOWAS states undertake to cooperate to maintain peace, stability and security within the region and to establish and strengthen appropriate mechanisms for timely prevention and resolution of conflicts in the region.

The revised Treaty also created an opportunity for the African Union's (AU) African Economic Community (AEC) and other AU instruments to be taken into account in the ECOWAS Treaty framework. This provided a basis for ECOWAS to be recognised as a pillar of the AEC, thereby establishing a link between the AU and ECOWAS, despite the fact that ECOWAS retains an independent existence. The 1993 Treaty also created a legal foundation for ECOWAS institutions to apply the African Charter as the benchmark of human rights for citizens under the Community framework. This fact is significant in the sense that the AU arguably constitutes an influence zone through which civil society can lobby ECOWAS organs and institutions.

Overall, the revision of the 1975 ECOWAS Treaty has expanded the focus of the Community from the narrow field of economic integration to a wider range of economic, social, security and political issues. Hence, the ECOWAS Commission announced that "ECOWAS is an organisation for political and economic integration, quite distinct from what is referred to as 'regional economic communities,' which have restricted their scope of intervention to the common market." Civil society can therefore validly pursue and support non-economic agendas within the ECOWAS framework.

3.1.2 Institutional reform in the ECOWAS framework

The 1993 Treaty revision resulted in the first major reform of the ECOWAS institutional framework. However, the revised Treaty retained the normative framework that existed under the 1975 Treaty. Thus, the Community remained an intergovernmental organisation depending on treaties for its governance. Under this regime, the ECOWAS Secretariat was essentially established to service the secretarial needs of the decision-making institutions. The focus of influence at this point remained with the member states. This changed in 2006 when major institutional and normative reforms took place in the Community.

In 2003, an ad hoc Ministerial Committee on the Harmonisation of Community Legislative Texts was set up to "endow the Community with modern legal instruments". By late 2005, a decision was taken to transform the Executive Secretariat into a Commission. This led to a large-scale amendment of the 1993 revised Treaty. Perhaps the most important institutional reform introduced by Supplementary Protocol A/SP.1/06/06 is the establishment of the ECOWAS Commission to replace the former Executive Secretariat. The new Article 17 provided for the offices of a President, a Vice-President and seven Commissioners for the ECOWAS Commission (see 3.2 Organs and institutions of ECOWAS and Table 3.2 for more detail).

ECOWAS Community Court of Justice

The 2006 institutional reforms also saw the adoption of a Supplementary Protocol on the Community of Justice. This Supplementary Protocol introduced major institutional reforms in the ECOWAS Community Court of Justice (ECCJ). Under the 1991 Protocol establishing the ECCJ, judges of the court are required to be persons with "high moral character and ... the qualification required in their respective countries for appointment to the highest judicial offices" or to be "jurisconsult of recognised competence in international law". Supplementary Protocol A/SP.2/06/66 adds that a candidate for appointment to the ECCJ should be competent in "areas of Community Law or Regional Law" and should have "a total of no less than 20 years professional experience". Supplementary Protocol A/SP.2/06/66 also reduces the term of office of the President and Vice-President of the ECCJ from three to two years.

Another innovation introduced in 2006 relates to the process of appointing of judges. Under the 1991 Protocol, judges were appointed by the Authority from a list of persons nominated by member states. Nominees were listed alphabetically by the Executive Secretary and forwarded to the Council. Appointment was made from a shortlist of 14 persons proposed by Council. By contrast, under the 2006 Supplementary Protocol, the Authority allocates vacant judicial positions to member states, and a Judicial Council made up of the Chief Justices of states other than those to which the offices have been allocated make the initial selection. The Judicial Council selects three candidates from each of the eligible member states, interviews the candidates and proposes their appointments to the Authority. Effectively, judicial independence is strengthened by the reduction of political involvement in the appointment process. Up till now, there is no clear evidence of civil society involvement in this process, even though civil society gets involved in equivalent processes at national levels. In view of the role now given to the Chief Justices, civil society, especially bar associations, can play a greater role in the process.

The 2006 Supplementary Protocol also established a Bureau for the ECCJ, comprising the President, the Vice-President, the oldest judge and the longest-serving judge. The term of office of judges was also reduced to five years by Supplementary Protocol A/SP.2/06/66. A final point to be noted is that the disciplining of judges and the determination of inability to perform the functions of judicial office has also been shifted to the Judicial Council. However, the ultimate power to dismiss a judge of the ECCJ still resides in the Authority, though it can only be exercised on the recommendation of the Judicial Council.

Community Parliament

In relation to the Community Parliament, Supplementary Protocol A/SP.3/06/66 repeals parts of the 1994 Protocol Establishing the ECOWAS Community Parliament and formally designates the legislative body as the ECOWAS Parliament. Articles 4 and 7 in Supplementary Protocol A/

SP.3/06/66 respectively establish a four-year life span for the Parliament and stipulates that parliamentarians shall hold office for four years from the day they are sworn in. Further, the Supplementary Protocol entrenches the political and administrative aspects of the management of Parliament. While political management is shared among the Plenary, the Bureau of the Parliament (Speaker of Parliament and the First, Second, Third and Fourth Deputy Speakers) and the Conference of Bureaux (the Speaker, the Chairmen or Deputy Chairmen and the Rapporteur of each of the Parliament's Standing Committees), administration is generally in the hands of the Bureau with the assistance of the administrative head of Parliament.

Technical Commissions

The amendment to Article 22 of the revised Treaty transforms the Technical Commissions into Technical Committees and establishes nine of those Committees along thematic lines:

- Administration and Finance;
- Agriculture, Environment and Water Resources;
- Human and Gender Development;
- Infrastructure;
- Macro-economic Policies;
- Political Affairs, Peace and Security;
- Trade, Customs, Free Movement of Persons;
- Legal and Judicial Affairs; and
- Information and Communications Technology.

National Units

Although it was not affected by the 2006 reforms, another ECOWAS institution that has undergone transformation over the years is the National Unit in member states. Based on a need to create structures in member states to ensure "the implementation and follow-up of acts and decisions of Community decision-making bodies", in 1983 the Authority approved a 1982 recommendation of Council that member states establish "National Units". The Authority also approved the establishment of a unit in the ECOWAS Secretariat to monitor the implementation of Community Acts and Decisions and collect information on the organisation of national structures set up by member states. In 1990, a decision was made to upgrade the status of these national structures to ECOWAS National Units in member states. This was followed by the 2005 Council Regulation C/REG.4/06/05 spelling out the mission, role and functions of the ECOWAS National Units. With the adoption of the vision to turn ECOWAS from an ECOWAS of states to an ECOWAS of peoples, in 2010 the ECOWAS Council came up with new regulations to provide guiding principles for the operation of ECOWAS National Units. Although they currently appear to be underutilised, National Units are important entry points for civil society organisations (CSOs) seeking to engage ECOWAS from the national level.

3.1.3 The ECOWAS legal framework

The first legal regime for ECOWAS adopted in 1993 was replaced by the 2006 regime. Of course, the legacy of the first regime remains. On the one hand, under the 1993 revised Treaty regime, the highest forms of Community obligations were contained in the Treaty, the Protocols and the Conventions adopted by the Authority. Thus, that category of ECOWAS instruments only come into force when the required number of ratifications has been reached and the ratification instruments have been deposited with the ECOWAS Commission. In that regime, CSOs can play a significant role in lobbying member states to ratify the instruments they have not yet ratified.

ECOWAS Protocols and Conventions are supplemented by Decisions of the Heads of States and Governments as well as Regulations and Decisions of the Council of Ministers. A number of

Protocols and Conventions currently exist as a major part of the ECOWAS legal regime and are useful instruments for the implementation of the Treaty. Some of these Protocols and Conventions have been ratified by the required number of states and have therefore entered into force. According to the ECOWAS Commission's own records, as at December 2011, no less than 38 Protocols and Conventions had entered into force. Some others have only entered into force provisionally upon signature – by a special practice of ECOWAS, certain instruments enter into force provisionally (temporarily) as soon as they are signed, pending ratification. As at December 2012 there were 12 protocols that are only in force provisionally. Others have not entered into force at all as a result of an insufficient number of signatures and/or ratifications.

Under the current legal regime, legislative instruments of the Authority are rechristened Supplementary Acts and stipulated to be annexures to the Treaty. The Council of Ministers is empowered to enact Regulations and issue Directives and Decisions. Supplementary Acts, Regulations, Directives and Decisions of ECOWAS therefore replace Protocols and Conventions as Community legislative instruments. Accordingly, Supplementary Acts are binding on Community institutions and member states, while Regulations are binding and directly applicable in member states. Directives are binding on member states in terms of the objectives intended, but member states retain the freedom to decide on the best strategies for the realisation of objectives laid out in Directives. Decisions are binding on all those designated in the instrument.

The current legal regime is intended to transform the Community into a supranational organisation with organs or institutions binding member states directly without the need for ratification of treaties, protocols or conventions. The ECOWAS Commission is also empowered to adopt Rules and Regulations for the purpose of executing the Acts of the Council and these have the same legal quality and consequences as the instrument to be executed. In this regard, the ECOWAS Commission also has some legislative powers. An understanding of the Community's legal regime is necessary for CSOs, as it will not only shape decisions regarding where to mount campaigns for legislation, but also lobbying for implementation purposes.

Under the new Article 12 of the revised Treaty, legislative instruments are required to be published in the ECOWAS Official Journal within 30 days of their adoption and signing. However, in practice this provision is not respected. Member states are also required to simultaneously publish those instruments in their own official journals or gazettes, because ECOWAS Acts, Regulations and Directives enter into force on the date stated in their text in so far as they have been published. Decisions are generally communicated to the person designated in the instrument and they enter into force on the date of such communication or notification.

Table 3.1 Decision-making tools and their legal effect

Legislating authority	Type of instrument	Legal effect
Authority of Heads of State	Supplementary Act	Directly binding on member states and ECOWAS institutions upon publication.
	Directives	Binding on member states in terms of stated objectives but states are free to choose best approach to realise objectives (obligation of result not of conduct).
Council of Ministers	Regulations	Directly binding and applicable in member states and binding on Community institutions.
	Directives	Binding on member states in terms of stated objectives but states are free to choose best approach to realise objectives (obligation of result not of conduct).
	Decisions	Binding on addressee stated in the instrument.
	Recommendations	Not binding but persuasive.
	Opinions	Not binding but persuasive.
ECOWAS Commission	Regulations for execution of Acts of the Council	Binding in the same manner as the Acts they seek to implement.
	Recommendations	Not binding.
	Opinion	Not binding.
ECOWAS Parliament	Resolutions	Not binding.

The new legal regime also empowers the Council of Ministers and the ECOWAS Commission to formulate non-binding Recommendations and Opinions, respectively. The ECOWAS Community Parliament is empowered to adopt non-binding Resolutions in conformity with the Treaty and other legal texts of general application to institutions of the Community. The Resolutions are forwarded to decision-making bodies of the Community for appropriate and further action. Declarations, Recommendations, Opinions and Resolutions form the category of non-binding sources of law in the ECOWAS legal framework. These instruments can be seen as "soft law".

3.2 Organs and institutions of ECOWAS

The revised Treaty creates institutions and empowers the ECOWAS Authority of Heads of State and Government to create other institutions necessary for the governance and functioning of the Community. The most important institutions and organs of the ECOWAS Community are:

- ECOWAS Authority;
- Council of Ministers;
- ECOWAS Parliament;
- ECOWAS Commission;
- ECCJ;
- ECOWAS Mechanism for Conflict Prevention, Management, Resolution, Peacekeeping and Security;
- Permanent Representatives of member states to ECOWAS;
- ECOWAS Bank for Investment and Development;
- Intergovernmental Group against Money Laundering in West Africa; and
- West African Health Organisation.

Table 3.2 lists the central ECOWAS institutions.

Table 3.2 The central ECOWAS institutions

Institution	Notes
Conference of the Authority of Heads of State and Government	
Council of Ministers	Consisting of the minister in charge of ECOWAS affairs, the Minister of Finance and any other minister
Community Parliament	
ECOWAS Community Court of Justice (ECCJ)	
ECOWAS Commission	
Specialised Committees	
Specialised institutions	ECOWAS Bank for Investment and Development West African Health Organisation West African Monetary Institute West African Monetary Agency
Semi-independent specialised agencies	Water Resources Unit (based in Ouagadougou) Youth and Sports Centre (based in Ouagadougou) ECOWAS Gender Development Centre (based in Dakar)
National Unit in each member state	

3.2.1 The ECOWAS Authority

Article 7(1) of the revised Treaty establishes the Authority as the supreme institution of the Community. The Authority is the most powerful and important institution in the hierarchy of ECOWAS governance. The Authority is composed of heads of state and government of the ECOWAS member states. Since ECOWAS began to implement the Supplementary Protocol on Democracy and Governance, military leaders and civilian leaders who are considered to have taken power unconstitutionally are no longer accepted as members of the Authority. This is a major departure from the early days when military dictators were the driving force of the organisation.

The Authority is a political institution and is the highest decision-making body in the Community, responsible for the general direction and control of the Community. The main powers and functions of the Authority are set out in the 1993 revised Treaty but more elaborate powers and functions are contained in the Protocols, Conventions, Supplementary Acts and other important documents. According to these instruments, the powers and functions of the Authority include:

- Determination of the general policy direction and major guidelines of the Community;

- Overseeing and supervising the functioning of other ECOWAS institutions;

- Following up the implementation of Community objectives;

- Creating other institutions for the ECOWAS Community;

- Taking all decisions in matters of conflict prevention, management and resolution, peacekeeping and security, humanitarian assistance, peace consolidation, trans-border crime control, small arms and light weapons proliferation, as well as other issues covered by the Protocol relating to the Mechanism for Conflict Prevention, Management, Resolution, Peacekeeping and Security; and

- Appointing the President of the ECOWAS Commission and other senior statutory officers such as the judges of the ECCJ.

In addition to the powers and functions set out in Article 7, other significant functions performed by the Authority include granting observer status to relevant CSOs/non-governmental organisations (NGOs).

Apart from the dedication that they show by attending sessions, in their capacity as the Authority, heads of state have acted decisively in enforcing certain aspects of the Community agenda such as peace and security and the building of a democratic culture in the region. The Authority has acted firmly in authorising and funding military interventions to preserve peace and stability in the region. Even more significant is the readiness with which the Authority has acted in cases of unconstitutional changes of government in West Africa. The cases of Togo, Niger and Cote d'Ivoire are all indicative of this trend.

Chairperson of the ECOWAS Authority

Article 8 of the revised Treaty (as amended by Supplementary Protocol SP.1/06/06) creates the office of the Chairperson of the Authority, which is held on a rotational basis, by alphabetical order of states, by a head of state or government who is "elected" for a renewable term of one year. Generally, ascension to the office of Chairperson is almost automatic. The only situations where a head of state who is due to assume office would not be elected are:

- When the eligible head of state opts to forgo his/her chance – in which case s/he needs to give notice of at least three months; or

- When there has been a *coup d'*état or any other unconstitutional change or retention of power in the eligible member state.

As the formal head of the ECOWAS, the Chairperson of the Authority is a first among equals and presides over the summits and sessions of the Authority. The Chairperson is empowered to invite any person to address the opening ceremony of sessions. This is space that CSOs can exploit to put pressing issues on the agenda of ECOWAS summits and sessions. For instance, in March 2011, CSOs in the region organised a "One Thousand Women March" during the opening ceremony of the 39th Ordinary Session of the ECOWAS Authority to demand, among other things, the cessation of human rights abuses against peaceful political protesters in Cote d'Ivoire.

The Chairperson acts on behalf of the Authority and exercises some of the powers of the Authority between sessions. A significant aspect of the power of the Chairperson is to convene extraordinary sessions of the Authority whenever the need arises. The Chairperson of the Authority executes instruments on behalf of the Authority in cases where it is not necessary to capture the signatures of all heads of state and government. Decisions of the Authority for instance are only signed by the Chairperson. The minister in charge of ECOWAS affairs in the member state elected as Chair of the Authority automatically becomes the Chairperson of the ECOWAS Council of Ministers. During the incumbency of a member state as Chairperson of the Authority, that state's representative chairs and presides over all the statutory meetings of ECOWAS for that year. A grant of 0.5% of the Community levy due from the member state that is Chair of the Authority is retained by that state for use by the Chairperson for the performance of his or her duties. The power of the Chairperson to convene emergency sessions is one that CSOs can exploit in situations where very pressing issues emerge, since only one head of state needs to be lobbied.

The Malian crisis

At the height of the Malian crisis in early 2012, the ECOWAS Authority imposed diplomatic, economic and financial sanctions on the leaders of the Malian coup. The imposition of sanctions was followed by the appointment of one head of state as the ECOWAS Mediator in the Malian crisis. Following wide consultations with different sectors of Malian society, including civil society, the Mediator reported an improvement of the situation in Mali. Consequently, the 2012 Chairperson of the ECOWAS Authority announced that he had the consent to lift all the sanctions imposed. This is an example of how the Chairperson of the ECOWAS Authority functions with indirect input from civil society. The Chairperson is therefore a power point of influence that CSOs should target for lobbying purposes.

3.2.2 The Council of Ministers

The Council of Ministers is established by Article 10 of the revised Treaty (as amended by Supplementary Protocol SP.1/06/06). Originally, it comprised two ministers from each member state (including the minister in charge of ECOWAS affairs where such an office existed). Since the 2006 reforms, member states can be represented by a maximum of three ministers – the minister in charge of ECOWAS affairs, the minister of finance and any other minister of the member state. The Council plays a major role in the management of ECOWAS. The Treaty gives the Council responsibility to see to the functioning and development of ECOWAS. The main powers and functions of the Council as contained in Article 10(3) of the 1993 revised ECOWAS Treaty (as amended) are:

- Making recommendations to the Authority on action aimed at attaining the objectives of ECOWAS;

- Appointing certain categories of statutory appointee of ECOWAS;

- Supervising the functioning of ECOWAS institutions;

- Recommending external auditors to the Authority for appointment; and

- Scrutinising and approving the work programmes and budgets of ECOWAS and its institutions.

The Council makes the recommendations on which the Authority acts. The collaboration between the Authority and the Council currently constitutes the de facto legislative arm of ECOWAS, as they jointly account for all legislative instruments in the ECOWAS legal framework. In reality, the Council is the driver of ECOWAS as it directly supervises the work of the Commission and other institutions and agencies. Further, the Council monitors the implementation of the policies and decisions adopted by the Authority. When necessary, the Council appoints ad hoc committees and working groups to undertake specific assignments.

The Council is also responsible for the appointment of statutory appointees (other than the President of the ECOWAS Commission and the judges of the ECCJ) and other ECOWAS staff. In relation to those statutory appointees that it does not appoint, the Council plays a major role in the selection and recommendation of candidates to the Authority, either at a formal or informal level. All Decisions and Acts of the Authority are generally based on the recommendations of the Council. Thus, the Council's sessions precede the sessions of the Authority to allow the Council to prepare documents for consideration by the Authority. In view of the enormous powers and influence of the Council, CSOs need to place greater focus on the Council and its activities.

During sessions, the Council receives and considers reports from the President of the Commission, the meeting of the Administration and Finance Committee, the Financial Controller and the Chairman of the Audit Committee. The Council also considers reports on the status of implementation of the tasks assigned to the Community's institutions, organs and agencies. As such, the Council directly supervises most of the ECOWAS institutions and activities. The draft agenda for sessions is prepared by the President of the Commission and transmitted to the Council along with relevant supporting documents before the session. This means that CSOs should be able to work with the Commission to put critical matters on the agenda of the Council.

The Chairperson of the Council comes from the same member state as the Chairperson of the Authority. Usually, the minister in charge of ECOWAS affairs in the eligible state is elected as the Chairperson of the Council. The Chairperson requests the President of the Commission to convene sessions of the Council and presides over such sessions. The Chairperson of the Council opens and closes sessions, conducts deliberations, summarises debates, and rules on points of order. In between sessions, the Chairperson in consultation with the President of the Council exercises the powers of the Council. The Chairperson is also empowered to invite any person to address the opening or closing ceremonies of the Council's sessions. This is another very powerful and important office to which CSOs ought to pay special attention.

3.2.3 The ECOWAS Parliament

The ECOWAS Parliament is currently established by Article 13 of the revised Treaty (as amended by Supplementary Protocol SP.3/06/06). However, the Parliament was only formally constituted in 1994 by Protocol as envisaged in the revised Treaty.

The Parliament considers itself to be the representative organ of the people of West Africa in the ECOWAS integration scheme. Although it is ultimately intended to be transformed into a Parliament with co-decision-making powers that will enable it to share legislative powers with the ECOWAS Council, the ECOWAS Parliament is currently a forum for dialogue, consultation and consensus and does not enjoy legislative powers. Members of the ECOWAS Parliament are drawn from the national parliaments of member states, though it is envisaged that eventually ECOWAS citizens will be able to vote for and be voted into the Parliament. Until the Parliament is constituted by people elected through direct universal suffrage, it only enjoys an advisory status. Under the existing arrangement, member states receive a request from the President of the ECOWAS Commission for nomination of their representatives to the ECOWAS Parliament. This request is usually made three months before the end of the legislative year.

Each ECOWAS Parliament cycle lasts for four years and ECOWAS parliamentarians hold office for four-year terms. The Parliament currently has 115 seats, which are allocated to member states on the basis of their population. All states are entitled to a minimum of five seats but states with larger populations are allocated additional seats based on their populations (Table 3.3).

The ECOWAS Parliament is empowered by Article 6 of Protocol A/P2/8/94 to consider issues relating to human rights and fundamental freedoms and make recommendations to the institutions and organs of the Community. The Parliament has introduced the idea of requiring representatives from member states to present a country report on a wide range of issues during its sessions. The report covers issues ranging from the state of human rights protection in the country to the state of preparedness of each member state for the envisaged economic union. For states in conflict, the report is expected to cover a situation report on the conflict. For instance, during one of the sessions in May 2012, parliamentarians insisted on an update on the human rights situation in the Gambia, with special emphasis on press freedom. Parliamentarians put the representative from the Gambia under pressure and even proposed that human rights be made a specific heading under the country report. While this may not currently mean much, it is a tool that could be developed into a formidable pressure point for demanding better adherence to standards on human rights and governance by ECOWAS member states.

Table 3.3 Allocation of seats in the ECOWAS Parliament

Country	Seats
Benin	5
Burkina Faso	6
Cape Verde	5
Cote d'Ivoire	7
Gambia	5
Ghana	8
Guinea	6
Guinea Bissau	5
Liberia	5
Mali	6
Niger	6
Nigeria	35
Senegal	6
Sierra Leone	5
Togo	5
Total	**115**

Under the current regime, the ECOWAS Parliament may be consulted for its opinion in areas of integration, including:

- Interconnection of communication links;

- Telecommunications systems;

- Energy networks, media communications;

- Public health;

- Education, youth and sports;

- Environmental policy;

- Community citizenship; and

- Respect for human rights and fundamental freedoms.

Parliamentary discussion papers, which form the basis of debate, are generally circulated to members at least 24 hours before the session at which a matter is to be debated, although it is not uncommon for papers to be distributed during the session. Country reports submitted by members on the state of affairs in their respective states are sent to the Secretariat of the Parliament at least a month before resumption of Parliament. The Parliament's Committees on Public Affairs and on Human Rights commonly deliberate on country reports before presenting their own reports to the plenary for adoption. While this is still a developing area, experiences from 2012 upwards suggest that it is becoming an important aspect of the life of the ECOWAS Parliament.

A major avenue of consultation is the current practice of parliamentarians discussing and making their opinions on ECOWAS issues known after the President of the Commission presents a Statement/Report on the State of ECOWAS to the Parliament. The Commission has also begun allowing Parliament to peruse policy documents that are to be adopted by the Council or the Authority. The Parliament is also becoming bolder, as evidenced by calls in 2012 for such policy documents to reach parliamentarians earlier to enable quality contributions. A concrete example of such consultation was the presentation of the ECOWAS Humanitarian Policy and Plan of Action to the Parliament's Committee on Human Rights. Although at present consultation is mostly symbolic, as already concluded documents are brought before Parliament, the signs suggest that it will gradually take control of the practice and demand a greater role in the affairs of ECOWAS.

Another emerging practice of the ECOWAS Parliament is the adoption of Parliamentary Resolutions targeted at different stakeholders. For instance, at the height of the Malian crisis, the Parliament adopted a Resolution calling on the Authority to apprehend and sanction persons responsible for disrupting the transition programme in that country. In recent times, the Parliament has also begun to host and co-host seminars and workshops on issues of interest to ECOWAS. For instance, in June 2012, it collaborated with the International Parliamentary Union and other stakeholders to organise a seminar on the campaign against child trafficking and child labour. Thus, although it is yet to realise its full potential as a major institution of ECOWAS, there are indications that the Parliament is growing in influence and will soon begin to play an important role in the affairs of ECOWAS. ECOWAS parliamentarians are also now included in official ECOWAS election observation and monitoring missions.

The Parliament is managed by a collaboration of the political and administrative divisions. The political division comprises the plenary (which is headed by the Speaker of the ECOWAS Parliament), the Bureau and the Conference of Committees Bureau. The administrative division is headed by the Secretary-General of the Parliament, who is assisted by a number of professional and other staff.

The ECOWAS Parliament and civil society

The goodwill of the ECOWAS Parliament has been explored by civil society in advocacy for implementation of decisions of the ECCJ. One of the major challenges that the ECCJ has faced in the exercise of its human rights jurisdiction has been in the area of state compliance with its decisions. This has been most prominent in relation to decisions made in favour of journalists. Concerned about the risk that non-compliance with its decision poses to the ECCJ, the Media Foundation for West Africa (MFWA) – an NGO based in Accra, Ghana – decided to involve ECOWAS parliamentarians in developing strategies and launching advocacy to sensitise stakeholders on the trend.

In July 2012, the MFWA and the ECOWAS Parliament organised a forum in Abuja to discuss the enforcement of decisions of the ECCJ and their implications for human rights, democracy and good governance in West Africa. The programme brought together civil society actors, academics, judges and other officials of the ECCJ to discuss the issues at stake. At the end of that meeting, a Declaration was adopted calling on all stakeholders – including the Commission – to take steps to ensure that member states comply with the decisions of the ECCJ. Although the Parliament did not drive the initiative, it was willing to collaborate and provided its facilities for the meeting.

3.2.4 The ECOWAS Commission

What is now known as the ECOWAS Commission was established in Article 6 of the 1993 revised Treaty as the Executive Secretariat of ECOWAS. In 2006, the ECOWAS Authority amended the 1993 revised Treaty to establish the ECOWAS Commission, which would be able to collaborate more efficiently with the AU Commission. In 2013, the same Authority decided on a new structure for the Commission. The ECOWAS Commission is the executive arm of ECOWAS and is responsible for implementing the Treaty and other legislative instruments of ECOWAS. The Authority retains the power to restructure the Commission as it deems fit.

President of the Commission

The Treaty empowers the ECOWAS Authority to appoint the President of the ECOWAS Commission for a single term of four years. The presidency of the ECOWAS Commission is rotated amongst member states. The occupant of the office has to be a person of proven competence and integrity. A general practice has been to appoint a top-level diplomat or a person who has previously held high national office as President of the Commission.

The President of the ECOWAS Commission is the principal officer of the Community, the chief executive officer of the Commission, the legal representative of the Community and the financial authorising authority of the Community.

According to Article 19 of the revised ECOWAS Treaty (as amended by Supplementary Protocol SP.1/06/06), the duties and function of the President of the Commission include:

- Coordinating the activities of ECOWAS Institutions;

- Managing the external relations of the Commission;

- Strategic planning and policy analysis of regional integration;

- Executing the decisions of the Authority;

- Implementing the regulations of the ECOWAS Council;

- Convening meetings of representatives of member states' high institutions to examine sectoral issues;

- Preparing a draft budget and work programmes for submission to the Council of Ministers;

- Supervising the approved budget and work plans;

- Submitting reports on ECOWAS activities to all meetings of the Authority and the Council;

- Preparing meetings of the Authority, Council, Technical Committees and ECOWAS experts;

- With approval of Council, undertaking the recruitment of staff other than statutory staff;

- Submitting proposals and preparing studies to enhance the functioning of ECOWAS;

- Preparing draft texts for approval by the Authority or the Council;

- Conducting the Commission's external relations, international cooperation, strategic planning and policy analysis; and

- Collaborating with National Units for the purpose of gathering useful information from national institutions to enhance the objectives of integration.

The President of the ECOWAS Commission is arguably the most powerful individual in the ECOWAS framework. As one commentator has observed, the President of the Commission "plots the course of ECOWAS", because the office initiates or at least has influence over all policy documents and legislative instruments that get to the Council and the Authority. The fact that all other institutions and non-statutory staff report directly or indirectly to the President of the Commission further amplifies the actual and perceived importance of this office.

It is important to note that similar to the financial benefits that accrue for those holding the offices of Chair of the Authority and the Council, there is a practice of making huge budgetary allocations to the member state that produces the President of the Commission. The allocation is supposed to enable the hosting of meetings in the home country of the incumbent President. However, one report has it that the allocated sums are hardly ever used, as ECOWAS ends up footing the bills through the National Unit office in the home country of the President. In 2012/2013, this became a sore point as Nigeria opposed the continued allocation of funds to that budget line as unnecessary wastage.

The Presidency of the Commission is a useful point of call for CSOs and NGOs interested in meaningful engagement with the ECOWAS Community. A crucial role that the Office of the President of the ECOWAS Commission plays in relation to CSOs and NGOs is that it receives applications from organisations seeking observer status and transmits communications from recognised organisations to the Council and other relevant institution of ECOWAS.

The office of the President of the ECOWAS Commission is also responsible for receiving documentation from CSOs and NGOs for transmission to meetings of the Council or to meetings of any other ECOWAS institution to which a given organisation has been granted observer status.

Vice-President of the Commission

The Vice-President of the Commission is appointed by the ECOWAS Council of Ministers. The Vice-President is appointed for a single four-year term upon recommendation by a Ministerial Committee on the Selection and Evaluation of the Performance of Statutory Appointees. The Vice-President acts on behalf of the President as the need arises, but has the main responsibility of coordinating relations between ECOWAS institutions and agencies, as well as relations with ECOWAS partners.

Commissioners

The Commissioners of the ECOWAS Commission are also appointed by the Council of Ministers. They are appointed for a single four-year term upon recommendation by a Ministerial Committee on the Selection and Evaluation of the Performance of Statutory Appointees. A state to which an office has been allocated nominates three candidates and the Ministerial Committee picks and recommends one of the three for appointment. The Commission has 15 Commissioners and a number of general and professional staff.

Departments

ECOWAS has 13 Commissioners, who head the following departments:

- Agriculture, Environment and Water Resources;
- Education, Science and Culture;
- Energy and Mines;
- Finance;
- General Administration and Conferences;
- Human Resources Management;
- Industry and Private Sector Promotion;
- Infrastructure;
- Macro-Economic Policy and Economic Research;
- Political Affairs, Peace and Security;
- Social Affairs and Gender;
- Telecommunication and Information Technology; and
- Trade, Custom and Free Movement.

The Financial Controller of an ECOWAS department has the rank of a Commissioner.

While all the departments of the Commission hold some promise for positive engagement depending on the thematic interest of a given CSO or NGO, the following departments are particularly important offices with which CSOs and NGOs should familiarise themselves:

- Political Affairs, Peace and Security;
- Human Development and Gender;
- Administration and Finance; and
- Trade, Customs, Industry and Free Movement.

The Department of Political Affairs, Peace and Security is responsible for addressing issues of governance and democracy in the ECOWAS framework. It also designs and sets the agenda for the peace and security architecture of ECOWAS. This makes it an essential department for CSOs involved in human rights and humanitarian intervention, election monitoring, and building of a democratic culture.

The Department of Human Development and Gender addresses issues relating to human development and gender in the ECOWAS framework. Accordingly, it coordinates the work of the WAHO, the ECOWAS Gender Development Centre and the Youth and Sports Centre. Most importantly, it is also the office that coordinates with both local and international CSOs, NGOs and intergovernmental organisations through the CSO desk. This office acts as the official liaison between the Commission and CSOs. However, the experience of organisations such as the West African Civil Society Forum (WACSOF) shows that CSOs can also directly contact and deal with the agencies and thematic committees of ECOWAS. In fact, it is recommended that thematic issues be brought directly before the relevant department, directorate, specialised agency or unit even though issues can also be taken up at the level of the Presidency.

The Department of Trade, Customs, Industry and Free Movement is responsible for monitoring the implementation of the Free Movement Protocols. Since these Protocols are among the ECOWAS instruments that touch on the daily lives of ordinary West Africans, CSO engagement in this area needs to be improved.

The West African Network for Peace-building

The ECOWAS Commission is the nerve centre of activities in ECOWAS. Accordingly, there is always space for CSO/NGO interaction with the Commission. This can occur when:

- The Commission puts out a call for proposals to allow CSOs and NGOs to bid for projects;
- CSOs/NGOs sign documents with the Commission for collaborative work; or
- A particular organisation takes an advocacy campaign to the ECOWAS Commission.

A few organisations have had such experiences with the Commission.

The West African Network for Peace-building (WANEP) was established in 1998 as a coordinating structure for collaborative peace-building in West Africa. After the adoption of the 1999 ECOWAS Protocol Relating to the Mechanism for Conflict Prevention, Management, Resolution, Peacekeeping and Security, the ECOWAS Commission (then Executive Secretariat) commissioned WANEP to conduct an assessment of ECOWAS conflict prevention capacity and to identify the training needs of ECOWAS in the area, with a view to enhancing the implementation of the Mechanism established by the Protocol.

In February 2004, WANEP signed a memorandum of understanding (MoU) with the Commission that committed WANEP to providing training, technical assistance and on-site technical support to ensure that appropriate structures were in place to establish and strengthen linkages between CSO networks and ECOWAS. A significant feature of the MoU was that it enjoined and committed the ECOWAS office responsible for peace and security to assist in getting access to relevant documents and key personnel for CSOs. It also sought to ensure ECOWAS political support to facilitate civil society participation in the programme.

The collaboration was carried further in 2005 when a follow-up project was commissioned between July 2005 and June 2007 to allow WANEP to assist ECOWAS in building a community-level early warning system in the member states. The MoU between the ECOWAS Commission and WANEP allows the CSO to sponsor a liaison officer position at the ECOWAS Commission to provide civil society input to ECOWAS peace and security issues.

Recognising the critical role that CSOs have in the functioning of the ECOWAS early warning system, the ECOWAS Conflict Prevention Framework (ECPF) adopted in 2008 stipulates that CSOs have a major role to play along with states. Thus, ECOWAS sees its role as one of merely facilitating "creative conflict transformation interventions by states and CSOs". Accordingly, the ECPF envisages that "Zonal Bureaux for Early Warning shall adopt a participatory regional approach in data gathering by building and strengthening cooperation with member states and civil society, including but not limited to NGOs, traditional groups, diverse interest groups, women and youth organisations." In this regard, CSOs are increasingly being involved in the official ECOWAS election monitoring teams.

Media Response in Ghana

In 2008, Ghana-based Media Response successfully bid for a donor-sponsored project at the ECOWAS Commission. The project was initiated to strengthen the capacity of non-state actors to enable them to play a more effective and relevant role in the ECOWAS integration process. This project allowed Media Response to carry out interventions aimed at strengthening media capacity and creating awareness on the regional integration process among the Ghanaian populace. Since 2010, Media Response has worked with the ECOWAS Commission to play a leading role in the formation, inauguration and maintenance of the Regional Integration Network of Non-State Actors.

The Media Foundation for West Africa (MFWA) is an independent NGO founded in 1997. MFWA is based in Ghana and focuses on the defence and promotion of the rights and freedom of the media. In 2009, MFWA began collaborating with the Communication Department of the ECOWAS Commission to enable it to develop a regulatory framework for freedom of expression and access to information in West Africa. MFWA's draft was reviewed by an ECOWAS meeting of technical experts on communication before it was forwarded to a meeting of ECOWAS Ministers of Information. The draft will pass through a few other stages and if it is finally adopted, it will be a Supplementary Act binding on all ECOWAS member states.

3.2.5 The ECOWAS Community Court of Justice

Although it was originally conceived as a tribunal under the 1975 Treaty, in 1991 the ECOWAS Authority concluded a protocol to constitute what is now known as the ECOWAS Community Court of Justice (ECCJ). Under the revised Treaty, the ECCJ is established by Articles 6 and 15 as the principal legal organ of ECOWAS. Under the 1991 Protocol of the ECCJ, it was only open to state parties and Community institutions. However, the 1991 Protocol has been amended a number of times since then, resulting in the opening of access to the ECCJ for individuals and legal persons such as CSOs and NGOs in matters alleging a violation of human rights. The most important of those amendments occurred in 2005 when Supplementary Protocol A/SP.1/01/05 was adopted to expand the jurisdiction of the ECCJ. Since then, the ECCJ has heard over a hundred cases,[5] most of which relate to allegations of violation of human rights within the territories of ECOWAS member states.

Composition

The ECCJ is composed of seven independent judges appointed by the ECOWAS Authority from nationals of member states. The judges elect a President and a Vice-President from among themselves to manage the affairs of the ECCJ. The President and Vice-President of the ECCJ are elected for renewable terms of two years. The Bureau for the ECCJ, comprising the President, the Vice-President, the oldest judge and the longest-serving judge, is its highest decision-making body.

Under the 2006 Supplementary Protocol, the Authority allocates vacant judicial positions to member states, and a Judicial Council made up of the Chief Justices of states other than those to which the offices have been allocated make the initial selection. The Judicial Council selects three candidates from each of the eligible member states, interviews the candidates and proposes their appointments to the Authority. Effectively, judicial independence is strengthened by the reduction of political involvement in the appointment process. The ultimate power to dismiss a judge of the ECCJ resides in the Authority, though it can only be exercised on the recommendation of the Judicial Council.

Although there are ongoing efforts to create an appellate division at the suggestion of certain member states, the ECCJ is currently a single-division institution. At its interaction with Permanent Representatives of ECOWAS member states and ECOWAS National Units in March 2013, the ECCJ got these latter two bodies to accept a recommendation to create the appellate division, create sub-registries in member states and commence a fund for legal aid.

Jurisdiction

Despite the fact that it considers itself to be in an "integrated relationship with national courts", the ECCJ is an international court and has the power to review allegations of violations of ECOWAS Community obligations. It is authorised to apply ECOWAS Community law in particular and international law generally. The ECCJ may either be accessed directly (in cases of alleged violations of human rights) or through referral by national courts applying the preliminary ruling

---

5   Judicial statistics of the ECCJ as at 6 March 2013 indicates that 147 cases were filed before the Court and that 88 rulings made by the Court. See T. Amene-Maidoh, "The role of the ECOWAS Court of Justice in the Regional integration process", paper presented at the ECOWAS Day celebration in Addis Ababa, Ethiopia, 29 May 2014.

option. Unlike most international courts, there is no requirement to exhaust local remedies before a prospective litigant can access the ECCJ in cases alleging violations of human rights in a member state. However, complaints submitted to the ECCJ must not be anonymous and must not have been submitted before another international court.

The decisions of the ECCJ are final and binding on all parties before it. Decisions of the ECCJ that involve monetary awards are to be implemented according to the civil procedure rules applicable in the state where the decision is to be executed. In the short period of its existence, the ECCJ has enjoyed a high rate of total or partial compliance with its decisions, even though the Gambia has failed to implement two judgments delivered against it. However, the Gambia has not declared that it will not comply, but has rather sought to supply reasons why it considers the decisions difficult to implement.

As recently as 2012, the ECOWAS Authority adopted a Supplementary Protocol on Sanctions against member states that fail to comply with their obligations under Community law. Judgments and decisions of the ECCJ are listed as ECOWAS Community obligations that will attract sanctions when they are not complied with. Article 77 of the 1993 revised ECOWAS Treaty authorises the imposition of incremental sanctions for failure of a member state to comply with ECOWAS Community obligations.

Since 2005, the ECCJ has been granted judicial competence over the following subjects:

- The interpretation and application of the Treaty, Conventions and Protocols of ECOWAS;
- The interpretation and application of the regulations, directives, decisions and other subsidiary legal instruments adopted by ECOWAS;
- The legality of regulations, directives, decisions and other legal instruments adopted by ECOWAS;
- The failure by member states to honour their obligations under the Treaty, Conventions, Protocols, Regulations, Directives or Decisions of ECOWAS;
- The provisions of the Treaty, Conventions, Protocols, Regulations, Directives or Decisions of ECOWAS;
- An action for damages against an ECOWAS institution or an official for any action or omission in the exercise of official functions; and
- Actions by individuals alleging the violations of human rights within the territory of an ECOWAS member state.

Access to the ECCJ is open to a corporate body that alleges that an act or inaction of an ECOWAS institution is in violation of the right of that corporate body. However, the practice of the ECCJ has been to allow CSOs and NGOs access to bring human rights actions on behalf of victims who would otherwise not have been able to access the court. Since the ECCJ attaches a victim requirement to individual access, the only situation where public interest litigation (*actio popularis*) is accepted (and even encouraged) is where collective third-generation rights (as against individual rights) are involved. Recent decisions of the ECCJ seem to suggest that there is an ongoing debate among the judges regarding the question of whether access should be extended to CSOs and NGOs in appropriate cases where individual rights involving several victims are in question. CSOs have a major role to play in helping to push for the implementation of decisions of the ECCJ by ECOWAS member states.

ECCJ interaction with NGOs and CSOs

As a court of law, the ECCJ's interaction with NGOs and CSOs is somewhat restricted. However, the ECCJ has allowed CSOs and NGOs to be directly involved in shaping aspects of its work. For instance, when the court made a decision in 2004 that under the legal regime of the 1991 Protocol individuals did not have access to bring matters before it, CSOs and NGOs actively campaigned for the amendment of the 1991 Protocol.

In 2009, following what the Gambia considered to be an unfavourable decision against it in the case of *Ebrimah vs. The Gambia*, a proposal was put forward by the Gambia to amend the 2005 Protocol of the ECCJ by introducing a condition that local remedies should be exhausted by prospective applicants before human rights cases are brought to the ECCJ. A number of CSOs and NGOs – including the Open Society Initiative for West Africa (OSIWA), the West African Bar Association (WABA) and the MFWA – mounted a sustained advocacy campaign that targeted both ECOWAS structures and selected member states to ensure that the proposal by the Gambia was defeated.

The ECCJ has also involved CSOs and NGOs in its sensitisation visits to member states. In October 2012, the ECCJ organised an international conference in Accra, Ghana, on the theme "Human Rights, Democracy and Good Governance: Role of the ECOWAS Court of Justice". Organisations such as the Centre for Human Rights, the University of Pretoria, WABA and MFWA participated at the invitation of the ECCJ. At the Accra meeting, a proposal was made for a CSO coalition to ensure an effective ECCJ. This proposal was included as part of the joint declaration adopted by participants at the end of the meeting. Work is currently ongoing to set up the coalition.

The ECCJ and public interest litigation

The experiences of the Nigeria-based Socio-Economic Rights and Accountability Project (SERAP) represent an important case study on public interest litigation before the ECCJ. In 2008, SERAP brought an action against Nigeria before the ECCJ, claiming that the state had violated the right of the Nigerian people to education, dignity, wealth, natural resources and economic and social development. One of the main objections raised by the Nigerian state was that SERAP was not a victim of any of the violations it alleged. Therefore, the state contended that SERAP lacked the legal standing (*locus standi*) to bring the action. In its ruling in 2009, the ECCJ accepted SERAP's argument that it was in the interest of human rights for the scope of public interest litigation (*actio popularis*) to be expanded to enable NGOs to bring action for the protection of human rights even when the NGO does not claim victim status. The ECCJ agreed with this position and ruled that allowing public interest litigation was necessary to "satisfy the aspirations of citizens of the sub-region in their quest for a pervasive human rights regime".

In contrast to its decision in the SERAP case, in the case of *Mrakpor vs. 5 Others*, the ECCJ ruled in 2011 that Godswill Mrakpor, a Nigerian citizen who had approached the ECCJ to prevent the ECOWAS Authority from taking military action against former President Laurent Gbagbo of Cote d'Ivoire, did not have the legal standing to bring that action. The ECCJ stressed that there was a victim requirement attached to its human rights jurisdiction.

In 2012, the ECCJ again addressed the question of *locus standi* in another case brought by SERAP alleging a violation of the right of the people of the Niger Delta to a satisfactory environment. Again, this action was brought against Nigeria and once again, Nigeria challenged the legal standing of SERAP. In this case too, the ECCJ ruled that SERAP could bring the action on the basis of a public interest to protect collective rights.

While the inconsistency lies in the fact that some of the rights invoked by SERAP in the first case such as the right to education are clearly not collective rights, it may well be that SERAP succeeded because it lumped that right together with other clear collective rights. In summary, it is safe to state that public interest litigation is allowed in cases involving allegations of violation of collective rights.

3.2.6 The ECOWAS Conflict Management Protocol

In 1990, while still under the legal regime of the 1975 Treaty, the ECOWAS Authority authorised military intervention in Liberia as a broad measure to maintain regional peace and stability by preventing the spillover of the war in that country into neighbouring states. That intervention in Liberia was to be the first in a line of other interventions that increasingly received the endorsement and approval of both the AU and the United Nations (UN). The intervention in Liberia also formed part of the trigger for the amendment of the founding ECOWAS Treaty.

After the adoption of the revised Treaty in 1993, ECOWAS was again forced to intervene militarily in Sierra Leone in 1997. In 1998, in the midst of the ECOWAS military intervention in Sierra Leone, the Authority adopted a Decision to give some legal basis to the ECOWAS military action. However, it was clear that ECOWAS military operations in member states could not be founded on a mere Decision. Accordingly, in 1999 the ECOWAS member states adopted Protocol A/P1/12/99 relating to the Mechanism for Conflict Prevention, Management, Resolution, Peacekeeping and Security (Conflict Management Protocol) to establish the Mechanism for Conflict Prevention, Management, Resolution, Peacekeeping and Security (the Mechanism).

As stated in its preamble, the Conflict Management Protocol (and by extension, the Mechanism) was partly motivated by the concern that "The proliferation of conflicts that constitute a threat to peace and security ... undermines ... efforts to improve the living standards of our people." The Authority expressed conviction that "There is a need to alleviate the suffering of the civil population and restore normalcy after conflicts or natural disasters." Effectively, the Conflict Management Protocol is the means by which ECOWAS develops its acknowledgement of the link between peace and security on the one hand and regional integration on the other. The Mechanism provides ample opportunity for CSO engagement in the work of ECOWAS.

According to Article 3 of the Conflict Management Protocol, the main objectives of the Mechanism are to:

- Prevent, manage and resolve internal and interstate conflicts;
- Implement Article 58 of the revised Treaty;
- Implement relevant Protocols;
- Strengthen cooperation in the areas of conflict prevention, early warning, peacekeeping operations, control of cross-border crime, international terrorism and proliferation of small arms;
- Maintain and consolidate peace, security and stability within ECOWAS;
- Establish institutions and formulate policies that allow for organisation and coordination of humanitarian relief missions;
- Promote close cooperation on preventive diplomacy; and
- Constitute ECOWAS civilian and military intervention forces.

In order to achieve its objectives, the Conflict Management Protocol stipulates that the Mechanism will be funded by allocations from the Community fund and contributions and donations from the UN, other international organisations and interested states. The Mechanism operates through four main organs:

- The Authority;
- The Mediation and Security Council (MSC);
- The ECOWAS Commission; and
- The Council of the Wise.

Apart from these main organs, the Mechanism is supported by other important organs including the ECOWAS Early Warning System. Although the Authority is the highest decision-making organ of the Mechanism, the Authority has mandated the MSC to act on its behalf.

The MSC is made up of nine member states. Seven states are elected by the Authority to serve for a term of two years. The remaining two members are the current and immediate past Chair of the Authority, both of whom are automatic members of the MSC. The MSC takes decisions on behalf of the Authority on all matters relating to peace and security in the West African region. Other functions of the MSC include:

- Formulating and implementing policies for conflict prevention, management, resolution, peacekeeping and security;

- Authorising and making policy decisions on all political and military interventions; and

- Approving and reviewing the mandate of ECOWAS missions to conflict zones.

The most comprehensive and most significant policy document that the MSC has adopted so far is the 2012 ECOWAS Common Humanitarian Policy (ECHP). The document "seeks to standardise the practice of humanitarian action in ECOWAS member states by fostering a balanced linkage between humanitarian action, human security and human development throughout the ECOWAS space based on the principle of regional solidarity." The ECHP formally documents the crucial paradigm shift in ECOWAS that has seen its focus move from exclusive concern about state security to a robust concern about human security. The ECHP also demonstrates the realisation in official quarters that CSOs can and do play an important role in sustainable peace-building and consolidation. Decisions of the MSC are taken at three main levels:

- Meetings at the level of heads of state and government;

- Meetings at the level of ministers involving national Ministers of Foreign Affairs, Defence and Internal Affairs; and

- Meetings at the level of ambassadors accredited as Permanent Representatives to ECOWAS.

The significance from a CSO perspective is that advocacy and other interventions need not be at the highest level but can occur at the level that is most accessible to any given organisation. At least one organisation – WACSOF – confirms that intervention at any of these levels of MSC decision-making can be very effective.

The MSC is supported by other organs such as the Defence and Security Commission and the Council of the Wise. The work of the MSC is further aided by the ECOWAS Early Warning System, which operates an Observation and Monitoring Centre within the ECOWAS Commission, and four Observation and Monitoring Zones located in four different ECOWAS member states.

Article 41 of the Conflict Management Protocol reflects recognition of the importance of CSO/NGO involvement in the ECOWAS peace and security architecture. It authorises ECOWAS to collaborate with civil society in implementing the Mechanism. It is at the community-level Observation and Monitoring Zone that CSOs such as WANEP have created opportunities for CSO input by appointing personnel to work with the ECOWAS national officials. There is insufficient material to assess the value of the ECOWAS–WANEP collaboration. However, some assessment of the overall success of the Mechanism is possible.

From the perspective of political will and ability to fully implement the Mechanism, there is some basis to conclude that the reaction of ECOWAS member states has been generally positive. By its own self-assessment, ECOWAS concludes that its conflict missions have been successful "as a result of effective involvement of decision-making bodies of ECOWAS".

By linking funding of the Mechanism to the Community Levy that is the main source of revenue, the Conflict Management Protocol reduces the risk of foot-dragging by member states that could have arisen had funding been left to ad hoc voluntary contributions by states. Although experience shows that the success of ECOWAS missions and operations under the Mechanism still depends to a large extent on voluntary contributions from states and funding from external forces, the core fund for mobilising these operations is within the immediate reach of the ECOWAS institutions. In 2011, ECOWAS had to await French support and intervention to engage in Cote d'Ivoire against Laurent Gbagbo even though the Chair of the ECOWAS Authority had already threatened to use "legitimate force" (i.e. take military action) if necessary. One consequence of this partial dependence on foreign financial contribution is that the possibility of ECOWAS intervention becomes tied to the interests of the donor states. Linked to this is the fact that the operation is partly controlled by those donors and there is a demand for accountability to the donors. While this demand for accountability is not necessarily negative, it could either create or reinforce the perception that the ECOWAS operations serve foreign interests, thereby undermining the legitimacy of such operations. There is also the further risk of inconclusive operations when the donor states give in to their own taxpayers' demands to withdraw support. Generally, donor funding has declined due to the economic downturn in the West and donor fatigue and this has further impacted on the size of the purse available to ECOWAS to fund the operations of the Mechanism. Another angle to the dependence on external funding is that CSOs that are able to lobby donor countries can successfully place pressing issues on the agenda by convincing donor states to tie such issues to the funding.

It is generally agreed that the ECOWAS Peace and Security Mechanism is the most advanced subregional mechanism of its kind. Arguably, the ECOWAS interventions in Sierra Leone, Liberia, Guinea and Cote d'Ivoire are examples of successful interventions by a regional organisation. In comparative terms, ECOWAS interventions stand out in most areas, including preventive diplomacy, military intervention and peacekeeping, as well as post-conflict reconstruction. Civil society involvement in some of these interventions has also been successful to some extent. For instance, organisations such as the Mano River Women's Peace Network (comprising women from Sierra Leone, Liberia and Guinea) are known to have played important roles in influencing action by ECOWAS during the civil wars in Sierra Leone.

In overall terms, the preventive diplomacy of the ECOWAS Mechanism has not been too effective – as the recent outbreak of internal conflicts in the region indicates. Although the Early Warning System may have been effective to the extent that some of these conflicts were anticipated and efforts were made to nip them in the bud, full-scale conflicts still broke out in Guinea Bissau and Mali. However, the ECOWAS preventive diplomacy in Guinea was arguably effective as then Burkinabé President Blaise Campaore's involvement in that country's presidential standoff averted a degeneration of the situation into open conflict.

It is important to note that civil society plays an important role in the Early Warning System, as civil society coalitions such as WANEP are actively involved in the ECOWAS warning system. It is noteworthy that within the framework of the ECOWAS–WANEP collaborative framework (ECOWARN), CSOs such as the Centre for Democracy and Development (CDD) and WACSOF have worked to build the capacity of CSOs and NGOs in the region to contribute to ECOWARN. Both organisations were also actively involved in the process leading up to the adoption of the ECOWAS Conflict Prevention Framework (ECPF). Clearly, greater commitment of CSOs can help to improve the system.

An important issue of concern is that the deterrent value of the system is still not fully developed, since national actors disrupt the democratic process in some member states despite the threat of ECOWAS punitive action. This limited deterrent value could be because ECOWAS lacks both the tool of effective sanctions (the freezing of bank accounts, denial of foreign aids, international travel bans, etc.) and the compelling threat of immediate military action. Notwithstanding all of these, ECOWAS is able to mobilise for military action by attracting the goodwill of other actors. This is why the ECOWAS Mechanism remains comparatively the most effective and most successful of its kind. The advanced collaboration between the ECOWAS MSC and the AU's Peace and Security Council is further testimony of the comparative effectiveness of the ECOWAS mechanism.

The Democracy Protocol

An important instrument that emanated from the Conflict Management Protocol but which enjoys an independent existence is the Protocol on Democracy and Good Governance Supplementary to the Protocol relating to the Mechanism for Conflict Prevention, Management, Resolution, Peacekeeping and Security (Democracy Protocol). Adopted in 2001, it entered into force provisionally upon signature while the necessary number of ratifications was being awaited. It is generally considered as providing the constitutional convergence for integration in West Africa. It addresses the human security needs of the peoples of ECOWAS. This instrument is important evidence of the recognition by ECOWAS of the link between democracy and good governance, peace, security, stability and integration. The Democracy Protocol is the legal foundation for election observation and monitoring activities of the Community. It is also through its provisions that the jurisdiction of the ECCJ was expanded to cover human rights issues.[6] It also encourages ECOWAS member states to establish national human rights commissions where none currently exists.

Based on the principles of constitutional convergence collectively adopted in the Democracy Protocol, ECOWAS has indicated a desire to "turn our countries into examples of vibrant democracies within which the fundamental human rights and freedoms of our citizens are sacred, respected and protected."

ECOWAS can be said to have done relatively well in implementing the Democracy Protocol:

- ECOWAS has successfully maintained its involvement in observing and monitoring elections in member states. While at times the argument has been made that ECOWAS election missions could be perceived as mere rubber stamps to give legitimacy to the ruling parties in the respective states, the refusal of ECOWAS to legitimise presidential elections in the Gambia in 2011 is an indication that such fears may not be totally justified.

- The promptness with which ECOWAS sanctions unconstitutional change of government or retention of powers in its member state far exceeds the experience in other parts of the world. ECOWAS sanctions in this regard have been imposed on political leaders in Togo, Niger, Guinea and Cote d'Ivoire.

Thus, the Democracy Protocol is a platform for CSOs and NGOs to build advocacy and other interventions aimed at building democracy and good governance in ECOWAS. As with the Conflict Management Protocol, the implementation of the Democracy Protocol is supervised by the Department of Political Affairs, Peace and Security.

Election monitoring, however, may be a touchy issue in the relationship between the Community and civil society. The tension that arose between the ECOWAS authorities and WACSOF over the 2005 political crisis in Togo is indicative of this point. In its Monitoring Report on the 2005 presidential elections, WACSOF reported that its officials were denied accreditation to observe the elections despite the active involvement of ECOWAS in the polls. The report says that whereas WACSOF saw the passing of former long-term President Gnassingbé Eyadéma as an opportunity to entrench real democracy in Togo, there was a feeling that ECOWAS was more willing to overlook flaws in the build-up to the elections in order to ensure that peace was maintained.

Notwithstanding incidents such as the Togo affair, CSO involvement in ECOWAS election observer missions is becoming increasingly robust as the Election Unit in the Department of Political Affairs, Peace and Security has made it a practice to invite CSOs and NGOs with an established focus on democracy-building and election monitoring to be part of such ECOWAS election observer teams. ECOWAS has also created a platform in the form of an ECOWAS Network of Electoral Commissions (ECONEC) to meet and share ideas and best practices. This creates an avenue for CSOs to interact directly with the electoral bodies themselves during ECOWAS election observer missions. Organisations such as OSIWA have been active in facilitating the activities of ECONEC and by extension, the ECOWAS efforts at building a culture of democracy in the region. For instance, OSIWA sponsors a programme officer to work in the ECONEC Secretariat in Sierra Leone, thereby providing an avenue for CSOs to get access to ECONEC.

3.2.7 Permanent Representatives

Until 2010, the role of ambassadors in the ECOWAS framework was essentially limited to participation in the functioning of the MSC. In 2010, the ECOWAS Authority validated the recognition of accredited ambassadors as Permanent Representatives to the ECOWAS Commission and approved the allocation of more concrete responsibilities to them. Accordingly, since 2010, in addition to the role they play in the MSC, Permanent Representatives are incorporated into the Technical Committee on Political Affairs, Peace and Security. Permanent Representatives are consequently recognised as vital links between the ECOWAS Commission and ECOWAS member states. They are

---

6   See Article 39 of the Protocol A/SP1/12/01 on Democracy and Good Governance.

expected to promote relationships between their respective states and ECOWAS institutions, just as they are expected to participate in the activities of the ECOWAS institutions to which they have been invited.

Significantly, Permanent Representatives are given responsibility for providing regular and up-to-date information on the implementation of ECOWAS obligations by their respective states. They are also expected to participate in ECOWAS sensitisation and advocacy programmes, and to advise their states on coordination between Ministries and Departments responsible for integration at the national level. Since 2010, to enhance their involvement in the ECOWAS framework, member states have also been encouraged to include their Permanent Representatives to ECOWAS in their national delegations to annual statutory ECOWAS meetings.

Some organisations, notably WACSOF, have some experience of engaging with the Permanent Representatives of individual states "when issues of specific relevance to the member state are involved". However, even WACSOF takes the view that at times engaging the National Platforms in the member state can be equally if not more effective. Notwithstanding these observations, the Permanent Representatives may be allies that CSOs find useful.

3.2.8 ECOWAS Bank for Investment and Development

The ECOWAS Bank for Investment and Development (EBID) and its subsidiaries – the ECOWAS Regional Investment Bank and the ECOWAS Regional Development Fund – were created by the amended Article 21 of the revised ECOWAS Treaty. Originally, the 1975 ECOWAS Treaty created an ECOWAS Fund for Cooperation, Compensation and Development as a financial instrument; it became operational in 1979. However, in a bid to "enhance the financial resources of the Fund through the opening of its capital to non-regional partners", the ECOWAS Authority in December 1999 transformed the ECOWAS Fund into the regional holding company EBID. EBID and its two specialised subsidiaries became operational in 2003 and are based in Lóme, Togo. EBID is supervised by a board of governors and run by a board of directors.

The objectives of EBID are to:

- Grant loans and guarantees for financing investment projects and programmes for the economic and social development of member states;

- Mobilise resources within and outside ECOWAS for the financing of its investment projects and programmes;

- Provide the technical assistance necessary for the study, preparation, financing and execution of development projects and programmes within ECOWAS;

- Receive and manage the portion of ECOWAS Levy resources meant for the financing of ECOWAS development activities;

- Manage ECOWAS special funds relevant to its corporate objective; and

- Carry out any commercial, industrial or agricultural activity, in as much as such an activity is secondary to its objective or necessary for the recovery of its debts.

EBID's cooperation activities take place within the framework of its corporate objectives. Thus, EBID cooperates with both national and subregional development organisations that operate within ECOWAS. EBID also cooperates with other international organisations with similar aims and other institutions involved in the development of the Community. Generally, the operational activities of EBID include project identification (in both public and private sectors), project appraisal and supervision, signing of loan agreements, and the disbursement and management of funds. There is, however, not enough material to engage in an assessment of its effectiveness.

In December 2012, EBID signed a part-financing loan agreement with the Société d'Exploitation Hôtelière du Togo, a Togolese public liability company. The agreement is for the sum of FCFA 5 billion[7] and is to be used for the construction of a 162-room, 4-star hotel complex in Lomé, Togo. The official position of EBID is that the "project mainly seeks to provide the Togolese capital with an international-class hotel establishment". The total cost of the project is put at FCFA 23.621 billion and it is to be financed "to the tune of 34% with own funds and 66% with bank loans". EBID explains that it "decided to provide funding support to [this project] as part of its private sector financing objectives, in accordance with the orientation of its 2010–2014 Strategic Plan".

Also in December 2012, EBID signed a loan agreement with Les Grands Moulins du Ténéré, a Nigerian limited liability company, for FCFA 1.550 billion for the acquisition of a flour mill, Les Moulins du Sahel in Niamey, Niger, through an assets acquisition mechanism, as well as renovating and upgrading the factory. This agreement was also part of EBID's private sector financing objectives, in accordance with the orientations of its 2010–2014 Strategic Plan.

3.2.9 Intergovernmental Action Group against Money Laundering in West Africa

The Intergovernmental Action Group against Money Laundering in West Africa (GIABA) was established in 1999. GIABA is the ECOWAS institution with a mandate that is closest to an anti-corruption body. However, GIABA's main responsibility is to facilitate the adoption and implementation of mechanisms to prevent money laundering and financing of terrorism in West Africa. GIABA operates from Dakar, Senegal, but has information offices in major capitals such as Lagos, Nigeria. GIABA is also responsible for strengthening the capacity of member states to prevent and control money laundering and terrorist financing in the region. It assists member states with establishing financial intelligence units and strengthening the capacity of existing units.

In addition to member states, GIABA grants observer status to African and non-African states, as well as intergovernmental organisations that support its objectives and actions and which have applied for observer status.

GIABA operates through four main organs:

- The GIABA Ministerial Committee, consisting of the three ministers responsible for Finance, Justice and Interior/Security from each member state;

- The Secretariat, which is located in Dakar, Senegal;

- The Technical Commission, which consists of experts drawn from the abovementioned ministries of member states; and

- A network of National Correspondents. Each member state is required to appoint one National Correspondent.

In 2010, an independent evaluation of the GIABA 2007–2009 Strategic Plan was conducted and one of the main findings was that there was a general lack of awareness about GIABA in the region. Accordingly, it was recommended that the agency develop a functional communication strategy. This has since been done and perhaps accounts for the increasing visibility of GIABA. CSOs are part of the listed target groups for the strategy and this indicates recognition that CSOs have an important role to play in the work of GIABA.

Among recent innovations in GIABA is the introduction of the Open House Forum in ECOWAS member states. GIABA also holds briefing sessions/meetings for ambassadors, partners and other stakeholders, as well as thematic workshops on issues ranging from money laundering to trafficking in persons. It is important to note that GIABA publishes its annual report online (even though not every year is covered currently). Although GIABA has been in operation for more than ten years, there is not enough material available to make an informed assessment of its effectiveness. It is hoped that this will change in the near future.

3.2.10 The West African Health Organisation

The West African Health Organisation (WAHO) was established by a Protocol in 1987 as a specialised agency. It is a merger of the francophone Organisation de Coordination et de Coopération pour la Lutte contre les Grandes Endémies and the anglophone West African Health Community, which had operated independently of each other in West Africa. Its objectives are the attainment of the highest possible standards and protection of the health of the people of the region, through the harmonisation of policies, pooling of resources and cooperation for a collective and strategic approach to the health problems of the region.

The main functions of WAHO are to:

- Study and promote research on the major endemic diseases of the sub-region and undertake activities aimed at eradicating or controlling them;

- Promote the training of postgraduate health professionals and where necessary sponsor the training of undergraduates;

- Advise member states on the health aspects of all development projects if requested;

- Collaborate with international, regional and subregional organisations with a view to solving health problems; and

- Propose conventions, agreements and regulations and make recommendations with respect to regional health matters.

Although WAHO is subject to the general supervision of the ECOWAS Authority and the Council of Ministers, it enjoys administrative and financial autonomy. The ECOWAS Assembly of Health Ministers has the specific mandate of shaping the general policy direction of WAHO.

3.2.11 ECOWAS National Units

Article 2 of Regulation C/REG.24/11/10 empowers each member state to create a National Unit to be responsible for coordinating and monitoring ECOWAS activities in that state. A typical National Unit should have seven staff members and be headed by a National Head of Unit with the rank of a Director. The National Unit is expected to be the focal point between the ECOWAS Commission and the member states and serves as the intermediary between ECOWAS and its sectoral departments on the one hand and national stakeholders on the other.

Responsibilities of National Units include:

- Facilitating the organisation of ECOWAS meetings and functions in member states; and

- Mobilising, organising and facilitating the participation of national actors in ECOWAS activities.

The regulation also creates a National Consultative Committee made up of National Units, Sectoral Focal Points, the private sector, civil society and other actors involved in the integration process. The National Consultative Committee is a forum for the exchange of information and the assessment of implementing of ECOWAS programmes. The Committee is supposed to meet once every three months under the chairmanship of the minister in charge of ECOWAS affairs in the state of his/her representative.

Member states are allowed to retain 4.5% of their Community Levy to fund the National Unit but the use of funds by the Unit is supervised by the ECOWAS Commission through the bi-annual report that Units are required to make to the Commission. CSOs have a right to participate at this level.

3.3 The decision-making process in ECOWAS

3.3.1 Meetings of the ECOWAS Authority

The most important meetings in the ECOWAS framework from a policy-shaping perspective are the Summits of the ECOWAS Authority. By Treaty, ordinary sessions of the Authority's Summit take place twice a year. One of the two sessions of the Summit is held at the headquarters of the ECOWAS Commission in Abuja, Nigeria. The second ordinary session of the Authority's Summit is hosted by member states on a rotational and alphabetical basis. As a rule, a member state is ineligible to host meetings of ECOWAS if the state is either under sanction by the Community or is currently under military or other unconstitutional rule. Although there is no fixed time frame within which sessions take place, ordinary sessions commonly take place between January and March and between June and August.

Extraordinary meetings of the Authority can be called as many times and at any time they are required. For instance, in the build-up to the ECOWAS intervention in Mali, several extraordinary meetings were held by the Authority. Extraordinary meetings can either be called by the Chairperson of the Authority or at the request of a member state. A request by a member state has to be supported by a simple majority of the ECOWAS member states. There is no fixed venue for extraordinary meetings but they commonly take place at the headquarters of the ECOWAS Commission. The quorum for meetings of the Authority is eight member states.

Although their opening and closing ceremonies are open to the public, all meetings of the Authority are closed sessions. However, when the need arises, heads of state and government may be accompanied by a minister or other expert to a meeting of the Authority, unless the majority of heads of state oppose this. It is also important to note that the Rules of Procedure for meetings of the Authority allow for any individual or organisation to be invited to address the meeting when the Authority considers it necessary.

The meetings of the Authority are normally preceded by meetings of the ECOWAS Council of Ministers, which also has the responsibility for drawing up the provisional agenda of the ordinary sessions of the ECOWAS Authority. Matters on the agenda of the Summit usually include proposals by member states. Decisions of the Authority are expected to be taken unanimously or by consensus. When it is impossible to reach a consensus on any matter, the Authority takes decisions by a two-thirds majority of members present and eligible to vote. By Rule 27 of the 2010 Rules of Procedure of the Authority, each member state has a single vote; however, member states under sanction are prevented from exercising the right to vote.

Arguably, CSO interventions targeted at Summits of the Authority are best routed through individual heads of state.

3.3.2 Meetings of the Council of Ministers

The ECOWAS Council of Ministers meets in ordinary sessions twice a year, on a date set by the Chairman of the Council after consultation with the President of the ECOWAS Commission and member states. Usually, as mentioned above, these meetings precede the Summits of the Authority. Extraordinary meetings of the Council can take places as many times as necessary. Such extraordinary meetings are convened either by the Chairman of the Council, at the request of a member state supported by a simple majority of other member states, or upon the proposal of the President of the ECOWAS Commission. Out of the two ordinary sessions of the ECOWAS Council, one is hosted at the ECOWAS Commission, while the other is hosted by eligible member states on a rotational and alphabetical basis. As with Summits of the Authority, a member state is ineligible to host Council sessions if it is under sanction or is currently under military or other unconstitutional rule.

Sessions of the Council are open to three accredited ministers from member states, including the ministers responsible for ECOWAS affairs and for finance. Ministers may be accompanied by a maximum of two experts. A minister may be represented by any other high-ranking officer designated by him or her. However, every delegation must include at least one minister.

The agenda for Council sessions is drawn up by the President of the ECOWAS Commission after consultation with the Chairperson of the Council. A provisional agenda and all documents relevant to the meeting are sent to member states at least 15 days before the opening of ordinary sessions. No time frame is fixed for sending the provisional agenda and relevant documents for extraordinary meetings but this is expected to be done in good time to enable states to study the documents before the meetings. Member states may also produce and submit draft Acts of Council, which may be transmitted to the Council through the President of the Commission. The provisional agenda usually includes items proposed by member states and usually comprises a section on items submitted for information only and another section on items for discussion and debate.

Council sessions have both opening and closing ceremonies at which public speeches are made. The Rules of Procedure allow for the Council to invite any person to address these ceremonies. Apart from the opening and closing ceremonies, the meetings of Council are held in closed sessions. Ministers may, however, be accompanied by their experts if there is no objection from the Council. The Council Rules also require that at least eight member states be represented before a quorum is formed. The President of the ECOWAS Commission is required to verify the accreditation and powers of accredited ministers before they can attend the meetings. Council decisions are expected to be unanimous or by consensus. However, if neither is possible, major decisions are taken by a two-thirds majority of member states present and eligible to vote. Each member state is entitled to one vote, whereas states under sanction are not eligible to vote.

CSOs can access the Council Summits through individual state delegations but also through the ECOWAS Commission; moreover, WACSOF has a statutory right to attend meetings of the Council of Ministers.

3.3.3 Meetings of the ECOWAS Commission

Meetings of the ECOWAS Commission are held at a departmental level on a bi-monthly basis or as circumstances may dictate. Meetings are held in closed sessions and deliberations are confidential. In what are considered exceptional cases, departmental meetings of the ECOWAS Commission may be addressed by persons who are not members or staff of the Commission. This is an avenue for CSOs who specialise in thematic areas to table pressing issues on the agenda of the Commission.

Draft policies and legislation generally emanate from either member states or the ECOWAS Commission. Drafts must necessarily pass through the Commission to specialised technical committees. Experts assembled by the Commission are usually invited to put finishing touches to draft instruments before they are sent for validation by a meeting of member-state ministers responsible for the issue area. It is after the validation and final vetting that the Commission submits drafts to the Council either for adoption (where applicable) or recommendation to the Authority for necessary action.

While there is insufficient material to sustain informed analysis on this point, there is a suggestion that the Authority has too little time to spend on policies and instruments beyond the general direction. As such, the most practical stages of decision-making to focus on are the Council, the Commission (Presidency of specific department or unit) and the Committees. At the member-state level, the National Units are considered to be the best points of contact.

3.3.4 Other meetings

Other important meetings of ECOWAS include the sessions of the ECOWAS Parliament. Only the parliamentarians, Members of Council, the Secretary-General of Parliament and staff of ECOWAS are admitted into the meeting rooms of the ECOWAS Parliament. People outside of this list cannot be admitted unless they have a badge issued to that effect.

The ECOWAS legal regime also makes provision for a meeting of a Committee of Legal Experts that is required to meet at least once a year. The Committee of Experts is expected to consider all proposals before such proposals are submitted either to the ECOWAS Ministers of Justice or the Council of Ministers. Meetings of the Committee of Experts can be convened by the ECOWAS

Commission on its own initiative or on the directives of the Authority or Council of Ministers, or even at the request of a member state.

The ECOWAS Commission also hosts meetings of the MSC of ECOWAS.

3.3.5 Influence zones in ECOWAS

The question of influence in the ECOWAS framework can be looked at from both external and internal perspectives. Internal influence can be disaggregated so as to properly understand member-state influence as distinct from institutional influences.

In terms of internal influence zones from the member-state perspective, population and financial muscle seem to count significantly in the ECOWAS framework. For instance, the allocation of seats in the Parliament is essentially a function of the size of a state's population (see Table 3.3). The financial contributions made by states also appear to influence the allocation of certain statutory offices in the Commission. One good example of influence that can be attributed to population size and strength of financial contribution is the decision to allocate a permanent seat to Nigeria as a representative of ECOWAS on the AU's Peace and Security Council out of the four seats allocated to the West African region.

Applying the size, population and financial muscle criteria, Nigeria, Ghana and Cote d'Ivoire traditionally stood out as the most influential member states. With the recent civil war in Cote d'Ivoire, Senegal has begun to emerge as the new leader of the francophone countries in ECOWAS. Burkina Faso has also been influential. Senegal's growing importance is resulting in a new alliance with Nigeria. Widely seen as the regional powerhouse, Nigeria plays a "Big Brother" role in the region – it provides approximately 70% of the entire funds of the Community and hosts all the major institutions of the Community.

The headquarters of the ECOWAS Commission and the ECCJ are located in Abuja, Nigeria. In addition to providing suitable accommodation and relevant logistical support for the offices, Nigeria also provides appropriately furnished and equipped residential accommodation for the heads of these institutions in accordance with the regulations guiding hosting of ECOWAS institutions. Nigeria is also generally the biggest contributor in terms of finances and personnel to the peacekeeping activities of the ECOWAS Community, often also providing field leadership.

In recognition of its contributions and as demonstrative of its influence, Nigeria is the only member state that is required to be represented permanently in the Commission even though it cannot claim any particular position permanently. However, Nigeria has never headed the Commission (in either of its incarnations); this, as well as the claim that the Nigerian quota for employment is always left unfilled, has generated some media reports that Nigeria is being short-changed. While this may appear unimportant, it could result in domestic pressure on the Nigerian government to reduce its funding of ECOWAS, which would present a huge challenge to the Community, as donors are not likely to be able or willing to fund the administrative costs of such a huge organisation.

Related to this prospect of Nigeria reducing its contribution by choice, there is also the question of the risk that faces ECOWAS in the event that internal political instability or security concerns force Nigeria to look inwards. This latter challenge is exacerbated by the fact that other member states are too small both individually and collectively to intervene effectively in a full-blown crisis in Nigeria. The recent spill-over effect of the Nigerian military onslaught against the militant Islamist movement Boko Haram in northern Nigeria, which forced people to flee to neighbouring states like Niger, demonstrates the danger that a destabilised Nigeria poses for the entire region.

While it appears that Nigeria wields huge influence in the Community, this influence is tempered by other factors. The most significant is the colonial–linguistic divide. Out of the 15 ECOWAS member states, eight are former French colonies with French as their official language – Benin, Burkina Faso, Cote d'Ivoire, Guinea, Niger, Mali, Senegal and Togo – while two are former Portuguese colonies with Portuguese as the official language (Cape Verde and Guinea Bissau). This leaves five English-speaking states – the Gambia, Ghana, Liberia, Nigeria and Sierra Leone – of which four were former British colonies. The tendency to date has been for the eight francophone countries to stick together on major issues, sometimes even wooing the lusophone votes. Hence, against the background that each member state has only a single vote, Nigeria and its English-speaking allies are outvoted. Part of the reason for this is that the eight francophone states are all also members of UEMOA and are thus able to take a common position on matters of interest. In this regard, Cote d'Ivoire, which has traditionally taken the leadership position among the francophone states, has acted as a major counterbalance to Nigerian influence. This ensures that unless Nigeria has a strong-willed leader who is able to throw his/her weight around by threatening to or actually withholding financial support for projects, it is unable to sway the direction of policy by the democratic process, since it will be outvoted.

An example of this bloc-voting is the fact that in the early stages of ECOWAS military interventions, the francophone countries have generally refrained from participating in the contribution of personnel and resources. The tension that can result from this colonial–linguistic divide is exemplified by the recent confrontation between the Nigerian Minister of Foreign Affairs and the President of the ECOWAS Commission. News reports suggest that first, Nigeria challenged the need to allocate funds in the budget to the home state of the President (who in this case is Ivorian) for the hosting of meetings, when the Community eventually pays for such meetings through the National Units. The standoff is said to have pitted the francophone states against the anglophone states, led by Nigeria. Second, Nigeria challenged the authority of the President to recruit staff into his office without the prior approval of the Council, resulting in extra expenses that the Council had not approved. Again, the matter was believed to have degenerated into a dispute along colonial–linguistic divides.

From the institutional influence perspective, the two most influential institutions in ECOWAS, apart from the Authority, are arguably the Council of Ministers and the Presidency of the Commission, in that order.

The bulk of decisions concerning the running of the Community emanate from the Council. This is because in addition to retaining the power of approval of the Community budget, the Council directly or indirectly supervises the work of all ECOWAS institutions and agencies excluding the Authority. The power of appointment, coupled with the requirement for institutions and agencies to submit reports to the Council, ensures that the Council has the loyalty of the heads of these institutions and agencies.

The Presidency of the Commission is also extremely important and influential, as the actual day-to-day running of the Community is its responsibility. As the authorising officer for all financial transactions by all institutions and agencies other than the Authority and the Council, the President of the Commission is able to exert direct and indirect pressure on the institutions and agencies of the Community. As the official representative of the Community, with responsibility for external relations, the President is the face of ECOWAS and is able to steer the course of the Community. A case in point is the open confrontation between the President of the ECOWAS Commission and South Africa over the ECOWAS intervention against Laurent Gbagbo in Cote d'Ivoire.

The powers of the President to put matters on the agenda of the Council (and by extension, the Authority), coupled with the supervisory power over the staff who draft documents and instruments, also mean that the Presidency can greatly influence the course of action at early stages of policy formulation. The legal experts and the Committee of Experts also have a big influence on policy formulation.

From the external influence perspective, international development partners play important roles in shaping decision-making in the ECOWAS Community as well. The influence of international partners is particularly marked in the build-up to the adoption of policy documents that ECOWAS has adopted in areas such as gender and migration, drug trafficking and human trafficking, as well as labour issues. It has to be recognised that by far the most influential external actor in ECOWAS affairs is the European Union (EU). The EU stands out as the region's main trading partner and it provides a major part of the foreign financial contributions to ECOWAS. In recognition of these facts, ministerial-level meetings frequently take place between ECOWAS and the EU. For instance, at the 19th ECOWAS–EU Political Dialogue, the EU raised important issues in areas such as peace and security, the fight against terrorism, and building and consolidating democratic governance in the West African region. Clearly, at these meetings, actors such as the EU contribute to shaping the direction that ECOWAS takes.

3.4 ECOWAS finances

In its early days, ECOWAS relied on contributions from member states and donations from development partners for income to fund its programmes. Since 2003, the contribution system has been replaced by an ECOWAS Community Levy that requires member states to deduct and pay 0.5% of all import value from the national level to the ECOWAS Community Fund. The change of revenue regime has also resulted in a significant increase in the revenue base. With the new regime (which shifts the focus from contributions to taxation), there are four main sources of ECOWAS income:

- Arrears from member states;
- ECOWAS Community levy at 0.5% of import value of member states;
- Donors'/development partners' contributions; and
- Special contributions by member states.

Under the prevailing regime, the level of dependency of ECOWAS has also been brought down significantly. ECOWAS 2014 budget was largely financed by its own resources, as about 95% of the budget was financed with funds from the Community levy, arrears and miscellaneous income, and only 5% funded by Development partners. The major contributions from the rank of development partners were from the EU, the African Development Bank, the World Bank and some bilateral partners.

Although the ECOWAS budgetary process is not generally open to external scrutiny and involves little, if any, external participation (creating an actual or perceived lack of transparency), it is possible to point out that the budget separates administrative and programme budgetary heads. Available documents suggest that, for instance, for 2013, ECOWAS budget planners had clear instructions to follow a strict ratio of 37:63 in favour of programmes in the preparation of the budget.

ECOWAS has put in place a comprehensive system of financial control. All departments contribute to the creation of the annual budget, but the final responsibility for its preparation lies with the Department of Administration and Finance. The ECOWAS budget generally comprises the following:

- A consolidated statement of income and expenditure;
- Separate budgets for each institution; and
- Separate sections subdivided into statements of income and expenditure for each budget.

Under Article 13 of the 2009 Financial Regulations of ECOWAS, the draft budget is forwarded to the Administration and Financial Committee for consideration and onward transmission to the Council for approval. The ECOWAS budgetary year runs from January to December. The President of the ECOWAS Commission is obliged to ensure that a draft budget is ready for consideration two months before the end of the financial year (i.e. October). In the event that a draft budget is not approved by the Council before 31 December of any year, the Council gives approval to the President of the ECOWAS Commission to continue to execute income and expenditure based on the budget from the preceding year.

The ECOWAS Financial Regulations provide for separate functions in the implementation and monitoring of budget implementation. According to Article 17 of the Financial Regulations, the offices and functions of the Authorising Officer, the Accounting Officer, the Imprest Holder and the Financial Controller are distinct, separate and mutually exclusive. The Principal Authorising Officer of the ECOWAS budget is the President of the Commission, although s/he may delegate his/her powers. The Authorising Officer is responsible for the sound and correct implementation of the budget and bears personal financial liability for intentional or grossly negligent actions that result in financial loss.

Each ECOWAS institution has an Accounting Officer, usually the head of that institution, who is responsible for the institution's funds. The Accounting Officer reports to the Authorising Officer. The Accounting Officer bears financial liability and is subject to disciplinary action for loss of moneys, assets and documents. The Imprest Holder – usually the Accounting Officer in each institution – bears financial liability in addition to being subject to disciplinary action.

Monitoring of the ECOWAS budget is the responsibility of the Financial Controller and the Audit Committee. The Financial Controller is an independent officer who reports directly to the Council, while the Audit Committee is a body appointed to assist the Council to ensure adherence to corporate governance in the ECOWAS Community. The Chief Internal Auditor of ECOWAS reports to the Council through the Audit Committee. The Financial Controller and the Audit team work independently of each other to ensure that the ECOWAS budget is properly implemented.

There are a few interesting points to note about the ECOWAS budget. Article 1 of Supplementary Act A/SA.1/06/07 Amending Decision A/DEC.28/01/06 Fixing Amounts to be used to Support the Activities of the Current Chairman of ECOWAS stipulates that an amount equivalent to 0.5% of the proceeds of the Community Levy payable by a member state holding the chairmanship of the Authority is given to the President of that member state as a grant to finance the activities related to that office and its assignments. Article 1 of ECOWAS Regulation C/REG.6/06/07 Granting Financial Support to the Member State Organising a Session of the Authority of Heads of State and Government grants financial support of 66,600 units of account to a member state that is hosting a session of the Authority. According to Article 2, even when the session is hosted by the member state that holds the Chair, the state is still entitled to both the Hosting Grant and the Chairmanship Grant.

By some estimates, about 60% of levies are paid by Nigeria, which also contributes up to 85% of total ECOWAS funds. This creates a feeling that Nigeria should have a major say in the allocation and use of ECOWAS funds. Other major contributors are Ghana and Cote d'Ivoire, in that order. For instance, for 2010, it was reported that Nigeria made a total contribution of USD 40.8 million, Ghana USD 14 million and Cote d'Ivoire USD 6 million. Development partners and some donor bodies have initiated a Pooled Fund to support ECOWAS institutions in a coordinated manner by setting up a programme-funding facility that the institutions themselves manage.

From a civil society perspective, the promise of ECOWAS funding for CSO engagement through support for WACSOF is an interesting initiative. However, little, if any information is currently available on the subject.

3.5 CSO and NGO work in the ECOWAS framework

With the adoption of its Vision 2020, ECOWAS resolved to increase the visibility and involvement of its citizens in the integration process. One of the main goals of Vision 2020 is to transform the organisation from an ECOWAS of states into an ECOWAS of people by 2020. This vision has brought about an increase in the actual room for participation of CSOs and NGOs in ECOWAS activities. Perhaps the most visible increase in actual participation is the growing involvement of WACSOF, as well as the increasing number of ECOWAS programmes aimed at creating greater awareness and involvement of civil society in Community affairs.

3.5.1 Forum of Associations Recognised by ECOWAS

Although the revised ECOWAS Treaty provides for the establishment of an ECOWAS Economic and Security Council to create space for active statutory CSO/NGO involvement in the ECOWAS framework, no such Council exists. Instead, in 1996, the Authority approved the establishment of an official coalition of NGOs and CSOs recognised by the ECOWAS institutional framework. The Forum of Associations Recognised by ECOWAS (FARE) is, in theory, the body established with the approval of the ECOWAS Authority to provide a platform for official CSO/NGO participation in the ECOWAS framework, with the following functions:

- Acting as a link between recognised associations;

- Providing a framework for regular exchange of viewpoints and experiences relating to the problems of integration; and

- Providing a focal point for the formulation of collective recommendations and points of view on prospective action for submission to the Council of Ministers through the Commission.

An indication of FARE's official status is that ECOWAS prescribes the modalities for the functioning of the body. FARE is expected to meet at least twice a year. Similar to other statutory meetings, FARE meetings are rotated between the ECOWAS Commission and the member states. Significantly, it is the Commission that has the responsibility to provide logistics support for FARE meetings. However, FARE activities are supposed to be coordinated by a bureau elected for a specific term of office by members of the forum.

Participation in FARE and its activities constitutes one form of CSO/NGO engagement with the ECOWAS institutional structure. However, there is little evidence that FARE is actually operative beyond the 2008 meeting that was held in Cotonou, Benin. In fact, there is a claim that FARE does not exist, even though no official confirmation of this claim was available from ECOWAS.

3.5.2 WACSOF

WACSOF appears to be the platform for actual CSO engagement with the ECOWAS institutions. After a first meeting of CSOs in May 2003 to address regional issues under the ECOWAS framework, two other meetings were held between CSOs, ECOWAS and development partners leading to the official formation and recognition of WACSOF as the platform for CSO engagement. By December 2003, WACSOF became established as an independent and autonomous body. Following the recommendation of a consultant, WACSOF was fused with the CSO Liaison Office within the ECOWAS Commission so that it emerged as the link between CSOs and ECOWAS. A 2005 Summit of the Authority held in Accra, Ghana, endorsed the idea of a more elaborate link with and involvement of CSOs in the ECOWAS framework. Accordingly, the Authority gave approval for the ECOWAS Commission to improve its support for WACSOF. The official support from the ECOWAS Commission basically came in the form of office space within the Commission. With such official endorsement, WACSOF enjoyed a healthy relationship with the ECOWAS Commission and was able to successfully make interventions at statutory meetings as well as ECOWAS meetings with development partners. WACSOF also receives financial support from the ECOWAS Commission every six years.

After a lull in its activities between 2007 and 2009 following internal problems, WACSOF resumed engagement with ECOWAS in 2010. The first major engagement after the lull was a meeting convened at the instance of the ECOWAS Department for Human Development and Gender to appraise the relevance and contribution of WACSOF to the ECOWAS project. This meeting was followed by other meetings, ultimately resulting in the conclusion of an agreement by which ECOWAS was to provide funding for the reorganisation of WACSOF as a forum and platform for CSO engagement with ECOWAS. Effectively, WACSOF may have replaced FARE, even though it is not an official ECOWAS institution.

Since its relaunch, WACSOF has been active in monitoring elections and monitoring the peace and security situation in the region. For instance, WACSOF provided a platform for a coalition of CSOs to follow the presidential elections in Togo. WACSOF has also been involved in other election observer missions (either as part of or independent from the official ECOWAS mission). WACSOF has also made statements on different conflicts in the region.

In recognition of its position as the platform for CSO engagement, WACSOF receives official invitations from ECOWAS through the CSO desk in the Department for Human Development and Gender to "make inputs in the work of ECOWAS on behalf of civil society in West Africa". WACSOF participation takes different forms, including participation at high level meetings such as the Development Partners Meetings, Council of Ministers Meetings, ECOWAS Parliamentary Sessions and Head of States and Government Summits. At such meetings, WACSOF is able to make statements on behalf of civil society. Other ways in which WACSOF presents the civil society position to ECOWAS are through the release of press statements and position statements/papers, advocacy letters and communiqués.

WACSOF's recommendations and other interventions are considered by the Council and a summary of those interventions is presented to the Authority for consideration. WACSOF attends all Ordinary Summits of the Community. For example, in the build-up to the adoption of the ECOWAS Reference Manual on the Culture of Peace, Human Rights, Citizenship and Regional Integration in 2012, WACSOF was invited to represent the civil society position. It also contributed to the ECOWAS Conflict Prevention Framework document. WACSOF also contributes to policy-making on ECOWAS military interventions through its involvement in military exercises.

3.5.3 Acquiring observer status

One of the main ways in which a CSO or NGO becomes recognised within the ECOWAS institutional framework is by acquiring observer status with the Community. Although the ECOWAS Authority had been granting observer status to organisations prior to 1994, the formal procedure for granting observer status was codified in 1994. The Decision codifying the procedure acknowledges that NGOs provide a channel for grassroots participation in the work of the Community and also reflect important elements of public opinion.

Generally, organisations with observer status enjoy certain rights and have certain obligations in relation to the ECOWAS framework. However, they do not have the same rights of participation that member states or ECOWAS specialised agencies enjoy. It must be noted that no organisation can be accredited with observer status with the ECOWAS Authority.

When applying for observer status, the applying organisation needs to show that:

- It is concerned with matters falling within the competence of ECOWAS;
- It has a constitution whose aims and objectives are in conformity with the ideals of ECOWAS;
- Its constitution provides for the determination of policy and for the election of a policy-making body;
- It is non-governmental and not under the control of any government;
- It is not a profit-making body;
- It represents a majority of the organised persons within the particular field of interest in which it operates;
- It has established headquarters with an executive officer;
- Its headquarters are situated in Africa;
- It has branches in at least two other African states;
- Its leadership must comprise nationals of African states; and
- Its basic resources are derived from contributions of its members, national affiliates or other recognised institutions.

The organisation is also expected to submit a certified report to the ECOWAS Commission every year stating the amount received and the names of donors of any voluntary contributions and financial contributions from any government.

Another important condition is that separate applications may not be made by organisations with common objectives and interest. This condition encourages the formation of coalitions by organisations working in the same or similar fields of interest. Where a number of organisations seeking observer status share common objectives or interests in a given field, they are advised by the President of the ECOWAS Commission to form a joint committee or other body authorised to carry out consultations with ECOWAS institutions. It is the joint committee that will be permitted to make a joint application on behalf of its members. Where such a joint committee has been granted observer status, no single member of the committee can separately seek such status.

(So far, the records show that the types of coalitions that have been granted observer status are mostly professional bodies such as the African Business Roundtable rather than regular NGOs.)

A major point to be noted is that national NGOs – NGOs that are registered to operate within the territory of a state – cannot be granted observer status with ECOWAS or any of its institutions. Instead, such national NGOs are encouraged to present their concerns through recognised regional NGOs to which they belong.

An organisation seeking observer status with ECOWAS or any of its institutions is expected to submit 40 copies of its application in each of the working languages of the Community through the Commission. The ECOWAS Authority may on the recommendation of Council withdraw observer status from any organisation if it gave false information in its application or if its activities are deemed to be counter to the aims and objectives of ECOWAS, or if there are other causes deemed by Council to be sufficient for the withdrawal of such status.

Organisations that are successful in their application for observer status with ECOWAS are classified as either Category A or Category B. An organisation is classified in Category A if it can show that:

- It has a basic interest in the activities of ECOWAS;

- It is closely linked with the social and economic life of the area it represents; and

- It has made sustained contributions towards the attainment of the aims and objectives of ECOWAS.

An organisation is classified in Category B if it is considered to have only a general interest in the activities of ECOWAS. However, there is room for review of an organisation's categorisation. In 2000, the African Business Round Table and the PANOS Institute West Africa were granted Category A observer status by the ECOWAS Authority.

A significant advantage of classification as a Category A organisation is that an organisation can be accredited to the ECOWAS Council of Ministers. Accordingly, such an organisation:

- Is permitted to send observers to all public meetings of the Council;

- May be invited by the Council to make an oral presentation;

- May through the President of the Commission circulate documentation to members of the Council;

- May be invited to collaborate with any committee as may be established by the Council;

- May (through the President of the ECOWAS Commission) submit questions or views for insertion in the provisional agenda of the meetings of the Council and of any other institutions apart from the Authority; and

- May consult with the President of the ECOWAS Commission on matters of mutual concern.

Category B organisations:

- Can be accredited to institutions other than the Council;

- May send observers to all public meetings of the institutions to which they are accredited;

- May circulate information, data or other documentation to the institutions to which they are accredited. Such documentation and communication can be placed on a list by the President of the ECOWAS Commission and be distributed to members of the Council upon the recommendation of the institution or at the request of Council;

- May be invited to consult with an ad hoc standing committee of the institution if the institution so desires or the organisation requests such consultation;

- May also submit questions or views for insertion in the provisional agenda of the meetings of the institution to which they are accredited; and

- May consult with the President of the ECOWAS Commission on matters of mutual concern.

Requests, documents and proposals submitted by NGOs to the ECOWAS Council of Ministers are considered by specialised technical commissions before decisions on them are taken by the Council.

The Regulations give the President of the Commission a major role in relation to the participation of recognised organisation in the ECOWAS framework. For instance, the President of the Commission has the responsibility to consider applications and request those with similar objectives and interests to form a joint committee. The President also has to consider requests from recognised organisations for changes in categorisation and consider reports and activities of the recognised organisations. In relation to Category A organisations, the President is empowered to consider requests from organisations for inclusion of an item in the provisional agenda of the Council. To do this, the President has to take into account:

- The adequacy of documentation submitted;
- The extent to which it is considered that the item lends itself to early and constructive action by Council; and
- The possibility that an item may be more appropriately dealt with elsewhere than by Council.

The President may:

- Distribute a list of documentation and communication from Category B organisations to members of the Council in appropriate cases;
- Hold regular consultations with recognised organisations; and
- Forward to member states all proposals relating to the granting or withdrawal of observer status before a meeting of the Council of Ministers.

A number of regional organisations currently have observer status with the ECOWAS Community and its institutions:

- West African Journalists Association;
- Federation of West African Associations for the Advancement of Handicapped Persons;
- West African Women's Association;
- West African Archaeologists Association;
- Pan African Federation of Film Producers;
- West African Sports Confederation for the Disabled;
- West African Enterprises Network;
- West African Union of Road Transporters;
- West African Youth Union;
- Federation of West African Manufacturers Associations;
- West African Subregional Committee for the Integration of Women in Development; and
- Association of African Jurists.

Despite the elaborate provisions on obtaining observer status with ECOWAS, organisations that have been engaging with ECOWAS do not necessarily have any official observer status with either the Commission or any other ECOWAS institution or agency. For instance, organisations such as CDD and OSIWA have successfully engaged with ECOWAS organs and institutions even though neither of these organisations enjoys observer status. Organisations that have participated in activities with ECOWAS institutions also confirm that they were able to do so without any official observer status. In each case, these organisations initiated contact with the relevant department and sustained engagement. This would then mean that whatever benefits there may be in it, a failure to acquire official observer status does not deprive CSOs of any possibility of engaging with ECOWAS institutions. Further, it has to be noted that although there is a procedure for acquiring membership of WACSOF, a non-member organisation is still able to contribute to civil society positions that WACSOF adopts on regional issues.

It appears that CSO/NGO involvement is more in the area of implementation than in the area of policy formulation. For example, in 2009, the Council adopted a Regulation authorising the President of the Commission to convene tripartite meetings involving representatives of ECOWAS member states, employers' associations and trade union organisations to address issues relating to the realisation of the ECOWAS Labour and Employment Policy and Plan of Action. The Regulation allows for representatives of CSOs and "relevant NGOs" and intergovernmental organisations to attend such meetings. The Regulation has been adopted as a Supplementary Protocol. The ECOWAS Regional Policy on Protection and Assistance to Victims of Trafficking in Persons in West Africa seeks to establish and maintain a supportive environment for victims of trafficking and commits to restore such victims to physical, social and economic well-being through sustainable assistance programmes. It specifically provides for the involvement of CSOs and NGOs in different phases of repatriation and resettlement.

3.6 ECOWAS and the African Union

The relationship between ECOWAS and the AU was formalised by the AU's 2008 Protocol on cooperation between the AU and RECs, which is informed by the recognition that the AEC and indeed the AU ultimately depend on the success of RECs, which are recognised as the building blocks of the AU and the AEC. Hence, in both the Constitutive Act of the AU and the 2008 Protocol, the intention is to strengthen the RECs. However, there is some uncertainty regarding the exact nature of the relationship and the RECs continue to maintain their independent existence. Nevertheless, ECOWAS and the AU have agreed to:

- Cooperate and coordinate their policies and programmes;
- Exchange information and experiences on their programmes and activities;
- Promote interregional projects;
- Support each other in their integration processes; and
- Attend and participate effectively in each and all of their respective activities.

For its part, ECOWAS has specifically committed to:

- Deepening its ties with the AU;
- Aligning its programmes, policies and strategies with those of the AU; and
- Integrating with other RECs in accordance with the relevant provisions of AU treaties.

As the legal representative of ECOWAS, the President of the Commission is in charge of all relations between ECOWAS and the UN, the AU and other RECs. ECOWAS and the EU have established liaison offices in each other's headquarters. This followed the signing of an MoU on Cooperation in the Field of Peace and Security between the AU and RECs that encourages the RECs to open liaison offices at the AU Commission. The ECOWAS office at the AU Commission has been in operation since 2008, even though the AU is yet to create a similar office within the ECOWAS Commission. Currently, the ECOWAS Liaison Office to the AU in Addis Ababa, Ethiopia, has severely limited staff strength and the ECOWAS Liaison Officer to the AU is believed to be experiencing challenges in the coordination and harmonisation of activities. The ECOWAS Liaison Officer attends all official meetings of the AU as an observer. She also attends the meetings of the AU ambassadors of the West African region. The Liaison Officer is also responsible for facilitating access for West African civil society to information on the relationship between ECOWAS and the AU, and more generally on the activities of the AU that are relevant to their fields of action. As a result of the limitations and challenges experienced by the office, limited activity currently takes place. Another reason may be the relative lack of information on the existence of the office such that CSOs and NGOs make few demands on it.

One area of active cooperation between ECOWAS and the AU is peace and security. As set out in Article 4(d) of the Constitutive Act of the AU, the responsibility for the establishment of a common defence policy for the African continent lies with the AU. However, in recognition of the fact that regional bodies such as ECOWAS have acquired structures for and experience in the area of peace and security, the MoU on Peace and Security between the AU, the RECs and the Coordinating Mechanisms of the Regional Standby Brigades of Eastern Africa and Northern Africa was adopted to ensure close coordination of activities.

Thus, RECs such as ECOWAS are expected to:

- Contribute to the full functioning of the AU's Peace and Security Architecture (APSA);

- Ensure regular exchange of information with APSA; and

- Develop and implement joint programmes and ensure consistency of REC activities with the objectives of the AU.

To ensure this, ECOWAS participates in meetings of APSA on behalf of its 15 member states. The ECOWAS MSC collaborates closely with the AU's Peace and Security Council, and ECOWAS-supported military forces constitute the West African brigade of the AU's African Standby Force. ECOWAS and the AU have collaborated in military missions in Cote d'Ivoire and Mali, among other places.

The lack of regular meetings between the organs and institutions of the AU and ECOWAS means CSOs working in the field of peace and security can enhance the level of coordination by targeting both organisations in their advocacy and lobbying work. CSOs are also more likely to be credible sources of initial information for officials of both organisations. The AU headquarters hosts an ECOWAS Day Celebration in Addis Ababa every May, which is an opportunity for dissemination of information on ECOWAS activities and interaction with AU organs and institutions based in Ethiopia.

3.7 ECOWAS's relationship with member states

ECOWAS relates with its member states at different levels. The President of the ECOWAS Commission is responsible for coordinating relations with governments and political authorities of member states through the intermediation of their Permanent Representatives.

ECOWAS National Units are the focal points between the Commission and member states and they:

- Facilitate the organisation of meetings at the national level;

- Coordinate the mobilisation of actors involved in the integration process;

- Promote the participation of the private sector, civil society and other stakeholders; and

- Ensure that member states honour their obligations to ECOWAS.

The National Units enhance ECOWAS visibility and strengthen the countries' participation in the implementation of integration programmes to ensure effective ownership. The Units are designed to function as relays between the Commission and the ministries concerned. However, the national political level seems to be the weakest link in the decision-making and implementation chain of ECOWAS. When it comes to personnel and material these units are poorly equipped and their allocation to specific ministries is rather arbitrary. In Senegal, for example, the ECOWAS unit is situated in the Ministry for NEPAD, African Economic Integration and Good Governance. Nigeria's unit is now part of the Ministry of Foreign Affairs; it had previously been in the Ministry of Integration, which has now been dissolved after receiving the lowest budget of all the country's departments for many years. The authority which harbours the unit in Burkina Faso is the Ministry for Economic Affairs and Development, which demonstrates the importance the country ascribes to ECOWAS.

3.8 Current debates in ECOWAS

Since its inception in 1975, ECOWAS has achieved measurable successes on all of its main mandates. In its nearly 40 years of existence, ECOWAS has put in place a series of regulations and institutions aimed at consolidating democracy and human rights, stabilising the peace and security environment, and harmonising trade regulations in West Africa. Despite these tangible achievements, huge challenges remain and these challenges must be fully resolved before the region can truly become an area in which democracy flourishes and where goods and people can move freely.

3.8.1 Peace, security and stability

Ensuring peace, security and stability in the region is one of the pressing challenges currently facing ECOWAS.

Despite creating the Conflict Prevention/Resolution Management mechanism, the ECPF and the Early Warning mechanism, ECOWAS has failed to prevent conflicts and crises in the region – as recent developments in countries like Mali, Guinea Bissau, Guinea and Cote d'Ivoire have shown. In all these cases, ECOWAS was not only unable to prevent conflicts, but has also been ineffectual in playing a primary role in their actual resolutions. If it were not for interventions from international actors (France, the UN and, rarely, the AU), some of the recent crises (Mali, Cote d'Ivoire) would probably persist. In the absence of efficient preventive diplomacy or an effective West African Standby Force, ECOWAS's ability to manage and resolve conflicts in the region is greatly undermined.

Terrorism, transnational and trans-border crime, drug trafficking, piracy, illicit financial flows, money laundering, corruption and human trafficking are also security-related issues of much concern for ECOWAS. Additional measures have been adopted by ECOWAS in an effort to address these issues – through such initiatives as the Counter-Terrorism Strategy and Implementation Plan in February 2013, GIABA and the West African Police Information System launched in January 2014 – but these have yet to prove effective.

3.8.2 Democracy and good governance

Another pressing challenge currently faced by ECOWAS is how to deepen democracy and good governance in the region.

In 2011, ECOWAS adopted its supplementary Protocol on Democracy and Good Governance, which established mandatory constitutional principles, including separation of powers, free and fair multi-party elections, and "zero tolerance for power obtained or maintained by unconstitutional means". Despite the democratic gains in the region, and ECOWAS interventions to ensure good governance in the region (election support and monitoring, the zero tolerance principle, preventative diplomacy and mediation interventions, etc.), ECOWAS still needs to take concrete and effective measures to deepen democracy in the region. This is especially true in terms of reinforcing the rule of law by strengthening the capacity of regional human rights institutions and by promoting participatory and internal democracy in member states. Democracies, good governance, access to justice and basic human rights need to be entrenched.

Considering the key role played by elections in consolidating democracies and ensuring accountability of governing elites and development, ECOWAS has been directing its efforts towards electoral processes. These efforts, however, should be complemented by contributions from civil society, and should cover the entire electoral cycle in each member state. ECOWAS should also increase its efforts to prevent electoral violence and ensure credible, transparent and fair electoral processes.

3.8.3 Protocol on Free Movement, Residence and Establishment

Another area of major concern is the effective implementation of the Protocol on Free Movement, Residence and Establishment. The realities faced by citizens in moving around the region sharply contrast with the promises contained in this Protocol. Its main objective is to improve the living standards of citizens through effective economic development.

Despite the positive impact seen in the past few years, challenges such as inappropriate border checks, rampant corruption, violence against and abuse of citizens by border officials, and the expulsion of nationals from other ECOWAS member states, must be addressed. To achieve this, ECOWAS has decided to:

- Introduce a biometric identification card as a travel document within the Community for ECOWAS citizens and a replacement to the Residence Permit issued by Member States;

- Revise the Protocol on Free Movement, Right of Residence and Establishment; and

- Redefine the concept of ECOWAS citizen.

Considering the instability in some member states, the protection and reintegration of displaced and refugee community citizens should also be a priority.

3.8.4 Economic growth, trade and the fight against corruption

Effective economic growth, development and the fight against corruption are also serious challenges for ECOWAS.

Considerable steps have been made by ECOWAS towards the harmonisation of its trade regulatory framework, but unfortunately these have not solved the majority of problems. The Common External Tariff (CET) adopted by ECOWAS was set up to standardise taxation on all imported goods in order to protect local producers and encourage local consumption. With the high level of informal trade and the relatively small economies in the region, the CET should guarantee the effective protection of national economies from other regions such as the EU. Another key consideration for ECOWAS is the disparity between economies within the region, which means it is essential that small economies such as Benin, Cape Verde or Togo are safeguarded to ensure they are not overpowered by "giants" like Nigeria or Ghana. Corruption also remains ubiquitous among institutions and citizens. ECOWAS will have to develop more innovative mechanisms to fight corruption in the region.

ECOWAS and the EU signed a comprehensive EPA in February 2014. However, the negotiation process was seen to be dominated by the regional ECOWAS Commission without space for national-level participation. Cape Verde suspended its participation in the EPA negotiations under the umbrella of the West African region and opted to negotiate a separate Association Agreement with the EU. Two ECOWAS member states, Cote d'Ivoire and Ghana, initialled bilateral Interim EPAs with the EU at the end of 2007/2008. Analyses of the interim EPAs reveal that they are bereft of development content and threaten West African regional integration.

It is feared that efforts towards an ECOWAS CET would be frustrated if the the EPA is not negotiated. Countries were concerned that several analyses have shown that EPAs will have negative effects on their economies, including a stifling loss of critical tariff revenues, deepened de-industrialisation and suffocation of small and medium-scale enterprises, the collapse of the agricultural sector, exacerbated unemployment, increased poverty levels, and regional disintegration.

3.8.5 Institutional framework

Last, but certainly not least, the weaknesses of ECOWAS's Internal Institutional framework are major challenges to be overcome.

The current ECOWAS institutional framework is designed in such a way that the Commission largely dominates all the other institutions – organs such as the ECCJ and the Parliament. These institutions need to be strengthened and synergies across all ECOWAS institutions must be developed. For the Parliament to be more effective, it needs legislative powers, which would take it beyond its current advisory and consultative role. More generally, it is worthwhile looking into enhancing the Parliament's powers through direct election of its members and how to provide oversight of the Commission's policies, decisions and actions. The ECCJ's powers also need to be enhanced – especially in terms of implementing a mechanism that guarantees the follow-up of its decisions and their implementation by member states. At the Commission level, the decision to have a 15-member Commission, with one commissioner for each member state, does not have a political basis. ECOWAS should be budget-conscious and avoid overlaps.

The financial autonomy and sustainability of ECOWAS are also major challenges and member states should contribute more to the ECOWAS budget to reduce its dependency on external donors such as the UN, the EU and others, as evidenced in the bloc's limited capacity to deploy its armed forces in Mali. All member states should contribute to the three main sources of ECOWAS income – arrears from member states, Community levy at 0.5% of the value of imports of member states, and special contributions by member states – in order to reduce donor/development partners' contributions. As ECOWAS contributions seem to be dominated by the richest countries (Nigeria, Ghana and Cote d'Ivoire), the other member states should try to increase their contributions to avoid the feeling that the biggest contributors' opinions hold greater sway over the others.

ECOWAS should also seek to have more of an institutional presence in its member states. This would make it more effective in ensuring implementation of policies. ECOWAS should also think about how member states can be sanctioned when they violate the institution's protocols and directives.

ECOWAS must further improve how it works with CSOs at both the regional and national levels, so it can develop closer, more effective and efficient partnerships.

3.8.6 ECOWAS 2020 vision

Achieving these objectives are top priorities for ECOWAS to reach its 2020 vision of building a democratic and prosperous community. For the institution to become "an ECOWAS of peoples", there must be a shift in its current strategy and policies. Its decisions and actions must become citizen-driven. If radical changes are not made in favour of a "people-centred" policy – its institutional vision to "create a borderless, peaceful, prosperous and cohesive region, built on good governance and where people have the capacity to access and harness its enormous resources through the creation of opportunities for sustainable development and environmental preservation" by 2020 may prove little more than a pipe dream.

Bibliography and resources

Articles and books

Adjolohoun, HS (2013) The ECOWAS Court as a human rights promoter? Assessing five years impact of the Koraou slavery judgment. *The Netherlands Quarterly of Human Rights* 31(3): 342–371

Alter, KJ, Helfer, LR & McAllister, JR (2013) A new international human rights court for West Africa: The ECOWAS Community Court of Justice. *American Journal of International Law* 107: 736–779.

Asante, SKB (1986) *The Political Economy of Regionalism in Africa: A Decade of West African States.* ECOWAS, New York: Praeger Publishers

Cernicky, J (no date) *What is the good of the ECOWAS?* Available at www.kas.de/wf/doc/kas_11781-544-2-30.pdf

Chinkin, CM (1989) The Challenge of Soft Law: Development and Change in International Law. *International and Comparative Law Quarterly* 850.

Ebobrah, ST (2012) Human rights developments in African subregional economic communities during 2011. *African Human Rights Law Journal* 223

Edi, EM (2007) *Globalisation and Politics in the Economic Community of West African States*. Durham: Carolina Press

Hillgenberg, H (1999) A Fresh Look at Soft Law. *European Journal of International Law* 499

Klabbers J (1996) The Redundancy of Soft Law. *Nordic Journal of International Law* 167

Michel, RR (2004) The integration of West Africa. *UE-L Journal of Undergraduate Research* 7(1)

Okom, MP & Udoka, EE (2012) Actualising the ECOWAS dream of a borderless region: Issues, prospects and options. *American Journal of Social Issues and Humanities* 117–132

Robert, R (2004) *The Social Dimensions of Regional Integration in ECOWAS*. Working 49 Policy Integration Department International Labour Office Geneva

Sall, A (2006) *Les mutations de l'integration des Etats en Afrique de l'ouest*. Editions l'Harmattan

Sesay, A & Omotosho, M *The Politics of Regional Integration in West Africa*. WACSERIES 2(2)

Sperling S (2011) *ECOWAS in Crisis Mode: Strengths and Limits of Regional Security Policy in West Africa*. Friedrich-Ebert-Stiftung, Department for Africa, Berlin, Germany

ECOWAS documents

1975 ECOWAS Treaty

1993 ECOWAS Revised Treaty

2007 to 2010 Strategic Plan of the ECOWAS Commission

2010 Rules of Procedure of the Authority

2010 Rules of Procedure of the Council of Ministers

2010 Rules of Procedure of the ECOWAS Commission

ECOPARL Session Dailies for 2012

ECOPARL Session Daily, 14 June 2012

ECOPARL Session Daily, 15 May 2012

ECOWAS Commission Annual Report 2009

ECOWAS Commission Annual Report 2010

ECOWAS Commission Annual Report 2011

ECOWAS Commission Annual Report 2012

ECOWAS Common Humanitarian Policy 2012

ECOWAS Conflict Prevention Framework document REGULATION MSC/REG.1/01/08

ECOWAS Official Journal, Volumes 1 to 58

Report of the Committee of Eminent Persons was appointed to review the 1975 ECOWAS Treaty (1992)

The ECOWAS Parliament's 2011–2015 Strategic Plan of Action

Websites

www.bidc-ebid.org

www.courtecowas.org

www.ecowas.int

www.giaba.org

African Union Documents

Africa, Our Common Destiny, African Commission

African Union Constitutive Act 2000

MoU in the Area of Peace and Security Between the African Union, the Regional Economic Communities and the Coordinating Mechanisms of the Regional Standby Brigades of Eastern Africa and Northern Africa

Protocol on Relations between the African Union and the Regional Economic Communities 2008

ECOWAS contacts

ECOWAS Liaison Office at the AU

Head: Ms Raheemat Momodu
+251 910 162065
raheematm@africa-union.org

AU Headquarters
Building C, Ground Floor, Roosevelt Street (Old Airport Area) / PO Box 3243
W12 K19, Addis Ababa, Ethiopia

AU Liaison Office to ECOWAS

Head: Ambassador Abdou Barry
+234 809 7314767
abdouab@africa-union.org

ECOWAS Secretariat
Plot 114, Yakubu Gowon Way, Asokoro District, FCT Abuja PMB 5368, WUSE Zone 2
Abuja, Nigeria

Gender, Youth, Sports, CSO, Employment and Drug Control

Director: Dr Sintiki Tarfa Ugbe
+234 703 4136011 / +234 805 9097083
sugbe@ecowas.int

ECOWAS Secretariat
102 Yakubu Gowon Crescent, Asokoro District, PMB 401
Abuja, Nigeria

4. The Southern African Development Community

Abbreviations and acronyms

AEC	African Economic Community
AfDB	African Development Bank
ASCCI	Association of SADC Chambers of Commerce and Industry
AU	African Union
BOP	Budget Outlook Paper
BRICS	Brazil, Russia, India, China and South Africa
COMESA	Common Market for Eastern and Southern Africa
CONSADC	SADC National Committee in Mozambique
CSO	civil society organisation
DRC	Democratic Republic of Congo
EAC	East African Community
ECCAS	Economic Community of Central African States
EPA	Economic Partnership Agreement
EU	European Union
FAO	Food and Agriculture Organisation of the United Nations
FOCESSA	Fellowship of Councils of Churches in Eastern and Southern Africa
FTA	Free Trade Area
GDP	gross domestic product
ICM	Integrated Committee of Ministers
ICPs	International Cooperating Partners
IGAD	Intergovernmental Authority on Development
IOC	Indian Ocean Commission
MIP	Minimum Integration Programme
MoU	memorandum of understanding
MP	Member of Parliament
RISDP	Regional Indicative Strategic Development Plan
SACU	Southern African Customs Union
SADC	Southern African Development Community

SADCC	Southern African Development Coordination Conference
SADC-CNGO	SADC Council of Non-Governmental Organisations
SADC-PF	SADC Parliamentary Forum
SAPSN	Southern African People's Solidarity Network
SATUCC	Southern African Trade Union Coordination Council
SGPA	Southern Africa Gender Protocol Alliance
SIPO	Strategic Indicative Plan for the Organ
SNC	SADC National Committee
UK	United Kingdom
UN	United Nations

4.1 Historical background and legal framework

4.1.1 The Frontline States and the Southern African Development Coordination Conference

The Southern African Development Community (SADC) was born out of the Frontline States, an alliance of countries that came together to fight against apartheid in South Africa. Its members were Angola, Botswana, Lesotho, Mozambique, Tanzania, Zambia and Zimbabwe. From 1977, active consultations were undertaken by representatives of the Frontline States on how to reduce their dependence on South Africa and so achieve economic freedom. These discussions were formalised by a meeting of foreign ministers of the Frontline States in Gaborone, Botswana, in May 1979, which called for a meeting of ministers responsible for economic development. That meeting was subsequently convened in Arusha, Tanzania, in July 1979. The Arusha meeting led to the establishment of the Southern African Development Coordination Conference (SADCC) in 1980.

The SADCC was launched in Lusaka in April 1980 at a Heads of States and Government Summit who adopted the Lusaka Declaration, "Southern Africa: Towards Economic Liberation". The original SADCC member states were the following countries: Angola, Botswana, Lesotho, Malawi, Mozambique, Swaziland, Tanzania, Zambia and Zimbabwe. They shared a common history of colonial experience, struggle for liberation, geographical proximity, people-to-people linkages and the corrosive effects of apartheid and racism.

A core group of the founding leaders were pan-Africanists well known to each other, who had worked together and supported each other in the fight against colonialism and apartheid. These were Kenneth Kaunda (Zambia), Samora Machel (Mozambique), Eduardo dos Santos (Angola), Julius Nyerere (Tanzania) and Robert Mugabe (Zimbabwe). Political solidarity became the main feature of the identity of the SADCC. It can therefore be argued that politics, rather than economic considerations, determined the establishment and functioning of the SADCC (1980–1993) and thereafter of SADC.

The SADCC and its member states were expected to embrace the following principles:

- Sovereign equality of all member states;

- Solidarity, peace and security;

- Human rights, democracy and the rule of law;

- Equity, balance and mutual benefit; and

- Peaceful settlement of disputes.

The objectives of the SADCC were:

- Reducing economic dependence, particularly, but not only, on the Republic of South Africa;

- Forging links to create a genuine and equitable regional integration; and

- Mobilising resources to promote the implementation of national, interstate and regional policies.

In deciding on the institutional framework, the founders took into account lessons and experiences from past regional cooperation attempts across Africa where the costs and benefits were not equitably shared among the member states, leading to disputes and disappointment. Within the region there was the experience of the Federation of Rhodesia and Nyasaland (today Zimbabwe, Zambia and Malawi), which was widely reported to have benefited Zimbabwe at the expense of the other countries. To avoid such an outcome, the SADCC from the very beginning placed particular emphasis on a decentralised institutional arrangement that would ensure that member states were the principal actors in the formulation and implementation of policy decisions.

It is important to note that there was no treaty establishing the SADCC. It was established by a Declaration. It focused on functional cooperation in key sectors with each member state given responsibility to coordinate a particular sector. This promoted decentralisation and identity of the SADCC at the member-state level. The number of areas of cooperation increased, as the membership of the SADC increased and also in response to new challenges like HIV/AIDS.

4.1.2 The transformation of the SADCC into SADC

With the end of apartheid and the transition to democracy in South Africa from 1990, there emerged the desire to move beyond solidarity towards regional integration. In 1992, nine heads of state of the member states (Angola, Botswana, Lesotho, Malawi, Mozambique, Swaziland, Tanzania, Zambia and Zimbabwe) signed a Declaration and Treaty that formally established the Southern African Development Community. The Declaration aimed at deeper economic cooperation and integration. The new Community had the following objectives:

- To promote development, poverty reduction and economic growth through regional integration;

- To consolidate, defend and maintain democracy, peace, security and stability;

- To promote common political values and institutions that are democratic, legitimate and effective;

- To strengthen links among the people of the region; and

- To mobilise regional and international private and public resources for the development of the region.

The Treaty of SADC aims at achieving common approaches and policies through Protocols in areas of cooperation. The Treaty was amended in 2001 to restructure its institutions and respond to new challenges such as poverty, gender, HIV/AIDS, globalisation, democracy and good governance.

Key features of SADC

The key features of SADC are:

- Centralisation of programme coordination and implementation within the SADC Secretariat;

- Twenty-one sector coordinating units grouped under four new Directorates:

  - Food, Agriculture and Natural Resources;

  - Infrastructure and Services;

- Social and Human Development and Special Programmes; and

- Trade, Industry, Finance and Investment;

- The establishment of SADC National Committees in the member states, comprising representatives from government, the private sector and civil society; and

- The adoption of the Regional Indicative Strategic Development Plan (RISDP), which sets out activities to be undertaken, with timelines, targets to be achieved and indicative cost, and provides a consistent and comprehensive programme of long-term economic and social policies.

The SADC region has a population of 277 million people and a combined GDP of USD 575 billion in 2012. South Africa is the dominant economy and a regional growth driver accounting for 71.5% of regional GDP in 2009. Angola, the second-largest economy, accounted for 10%, while the other ten countries contributed 18.5% to the regional GDP. The headquarters of the Secretariat are based in Gaborone, Botswana.

Table 4.1 Key SADC historical events

Date	Event
May 1979	Meeting of Ministers of Foreign Affairs of the Frontline States held in Gaborone, Botswana
July 1979	Meeting of ministers responsible for economic development held in Arusha, Tanzania
April 1980	The Southern African Development Coordination Conference (SADCC) formed in Lusaka, Zambia
January 1990	Namibia joins the SADCC
August 1992	The SADCC transformed into the Southern African Development Community (SADC) with the signing of the Declaration and Treaty of SADC at a Heads of State and Government Summit in Windhoek, Namibia
September 1994	Following the end of apartheid, South Africa joins SADC at the Heads of State Summit in Gaborone, Botswana
August 1995	Mauritius joins SADC
September 1997	The Seychelles and the Democratic Republic of Congo join SADC
January 1999	Decision to develop the Regional Indicative Strategic Development Plan (RISDP) made at a Summit of Heads of State and Government in Maputo, Mozambique
January 2004	Strategic Indicative Plan for the Organ (SIPO) launched
July 2004	Seychelles withdraws from SADC
August 2005	Madagascar joins SADC
January 2008	SADC, along with the Common Market for Eastern and Southern Africa (COMESA) and the East African Community (EAC), announce that they will be establishing the Africa Free Trade Zone
August 2008	Seychelles re-joins SADC
August 2010	SADC Tribunal suspended

4.1.3 Membership and legal frameworks

SADC membership

SADC has 15 members, with Namibia joining in 1990, South Africa in 1994, Mauritius in 1995, Seychelles and the Democratic Republic of Congo (DRC) in 1997, and Madagascar in 2005. Madagascar was suspended by the SADC Extraordinary Summit of March 2009 held in Swaziland following the coup by Andry Rajoelina that unseated Marc Ravalomanana's elected government. Acceptance of new members is based on unanimous decision by all member states at a Summit.

Article 37 of the Treaty stipulates the working languages of the Community as English and Portuguese. The Council is mandated to determine other official languages. French has not yet been designated as an additional language to accommodate French-speaking member states (Mauritius, Seychelles and Madagascar). The official SADC website lists French and Portuguese language options. However, these are not yet operational. Most SADC documents are only available in English.

SADC's vision and mission

SADC's vision is that of a common future within a regional community that will ensure economic well-being, improvement of standards of living and quality of life, freedom and social justice and peace and security for the peoples of southern Africa.

SADC's mission is to promote sustainable and equitable economic growth and socio-economic development through efficient productive systems, deeper cooperation and integration, good governance, and durable peace and security, so that the region emerges as a competitive and effective player in international relations and the world economy.

4.1.4 The SADC legal framework

The SADC Treaty

The Treaty is the founding document of SADC. In addition, there are Protocols, Charters, Declarations and other subsidiary documents that include model laws and policies. The Protocols are an integral part of the Treaty and are legally binding on member states. Disputes that arise in relation to the interpretation of the Treaty and Protocols are referred to the SADC Tribunal. The Treaty has been amended several times. Some of the key amendments are the centralisation and implementation of SADC programmes by the Secretariat, setting up of SADC National Committees and the inclusion of key stakeholders. Table 4.2 shows the key revisions that have taken place.

Table 4.2 Amendments to the SADC Treaty

Date	Nature of amendment	Description
2001	Agreement amending the Treaty	Amends the preamble and table of contents, with additional Articles on SADC membership and the Troika
2007	Agreement amending Article 22 of the Treaty	Describes conditions for an amendment to a Protocol
2008	Agreement Amending the Treaty of SADC	Describes the establishment of Sectoral Ministerial Committees and the SADC executive management roles
2009	Agreement amending Articles 10 and 14 of the Treaty	Outlines the structure and appointment of the executive management of the SADC Secretariat
2009	Agreement amending Article 10A of the Treaty	Describes the composition of the Ministerial Committee responsible for coordinating the work of the organ and its structures

The Treaty is a legally binding and all-encompassing instrument by which countries of the region are to coordinate, harmonise and rationalise their policies and strategies for sustainable development. Article 4 of the Treaty commits member states to respect:

- The sovereign equality of member states;
- Solidarity, peace and security;
- Human rights, democracy and rule of law; and
- Equity, balance and mutual benefit.

Article 6(5) of the Treaty requires member states to domesticate the Treaty by "taking all necessary steps to accord this Treaty the force of national law". In addition, Article 22(3) states, "Each Protocol shall be subject to signature and ratification by the parties thereto." The Decisions and Agreements entered into under the auspices of SADC are legally binding and require the member states to comply by incorporating legal provisions into national laws. Model laws, policies, strategies and plans are supposed to promote harmonisation at the level of member states.

Article 33 provides for sanctions to be imposed against member states that:

- Persistently fail, without good reason, to fulfil obligations assumed under the Treaty;
- Implement policies that undermine the principles and objectives of SADC; and

- Are in arrears for more than one year in the payment of contributions to SADC for reasons other than those caused by natural calamity or exceptional circumstances that gravely affect their economies, and have not secured the dispensation of the Summit.

The sanctions are referred to the Summit and determined on a case-by-case basis.

Article 21 of the Treaty provides for Protocol-based cooperation among member states. In accordance with Article 21(2), cooperation is through adoption of legal, institutional and implementation frameworks. Protocols are developed and adopted in each area of cooperation. These include

- Infrastructure and services;
- Economic and industrial policy;
- Natural resources; and
- Social and human development.

The Protocols promote legal and political cooperation. They also create structures that are coordinated by various directorates at the SADC Secretariat to implement the Protocols. The Protocols are approved by the Council of Ministers and signed by the Heads of State or Government Summit. The development of the Protocols is informed by international and continental agreements. Thus, once they are adopted, the Treaty requires that they should be registered with the United Nations (UN) and the African Union (AU). This is also in compliance with the Charter of the UN, Article 52, which provides that regional arrangements shall be consistent with the purposes and principles of the UN.

SADC protocols

Table 4.3 sets out the protocols signed by member states to date.

Table 4.3 SADC Protocols signed by member states

Protocol	Themes	Date adopted	Entry into force
Protocol Against Corruption	Politics, defence and security, politics and diplomacy	14 August 2001	6 August 2003
Protocol on Combating Illicit Drug Trafficking in the Southern African Region	Legal	24 August 1996	20 March 1999
Protocol on Culture, Information and Sport	Culture	14 August 2001	7 January 2006
Protocol on Education and Training	Social and human development, education and skills development	8 September 1997	31 July 2000
Protocol on Energy	Infrastructure, energy	24 August 1996	17 April 1998
Protocol on Extradition	Politics, defence and security, public security	3 March 2002	1 September 2006
Protocol on Facilitation of Movement of Persons	Politics, defence and security, public security	18 August 2005	Not yet in force
Protocol on Finance and Investment	Economic development, trade, industry, finance, investment, private sector	1 August 1996	25 January 2001
Protocol on Fisheries	Agriculture and food security, fisheries	14 August 2001	8 August 2003
Protocol on Gender and Development	Gender	17 August 2008	March 2013
Protocol on Health	Disaster risk management, health, pharmaceuticals, communicable diseases, non-communicable diseases, social and human development	18 August 1999	18 August 2004
Protocol on Legal Affairs	Legal	7 August 2000	1 September 2006

Protocol	Themes	Date adopted	Entry into force
Protocol on Mining	Economic development, trade, industry, private sector, social and human development, employment and labour	8 September 1997	10 February 2000
Protocol on Politics, Defence and Security Cooperation	Politics, defence and security, politics and diplomacy, defence, police, state security, regional peacekeeping, disaster risk management	14 August 2001	2 March 2004
Protocol on Science, Technology and Innovation	Science and technology, information and communication	17 August 2008	Not yet in force
Protocol on Shared Watercourse Systems in the Southern African Region	Infrastructure, water and sanitation, natural resources, water	7 August 2000	Not yet in force
Protocol on the Control of Firearms, Ammunition and Other Related Materials	Politics, defence and security, public security	14 August 2001	8 November 2004
Protocol on the Development of Tourism	Private sector, industry, tourism	14 September 2009	26 November 2012
Protocol on the Tribunal and the Rules of Procedure Thereof	Legal	7 August 2000	14 August 2005
Protocol on Transport, Communications and Meteorology	Infrastructure, meteorology, information and communication technology, transport, maritime, ports and inland waterways, meteorology and climate	24 August 1996	1 July 1998
Protocol on Wildlife Conservation and Law Enforcement	Agriculture, food security, trans-frontier conservation areas, wildlife	14 August 1990	30 November 2003
Protocol to the Treaty Establishing SADC on Immunities and Privileges	Legal, financial	17 August 1992	30 September 1993
Revised Protocol on Shared Watercourses	Infrastructure, water and sanitation, natural resources, water	24 August 1996	25 January 2000

Figure 4.1 Key Protocols and how many member states ratified them

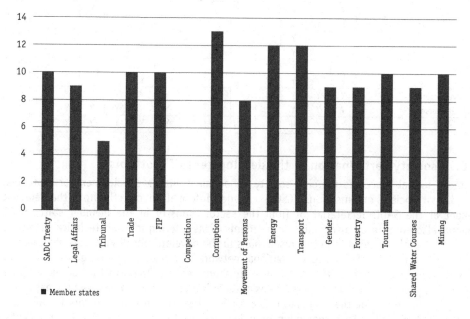

■ Member states

Figure 4.2 Number of Protocols signed by each member state

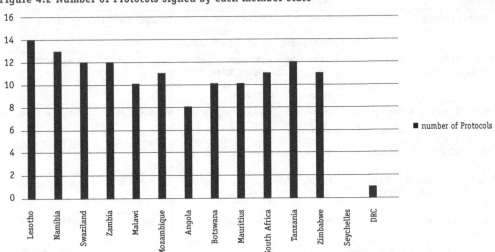

Table 4.4 A sample of ratification of SADC Protocols by country (Y = Yes, N = No)

	Lesotho	Namibia	Swaziland	Zambia	Malawi	Mozambique	Angola	Botswana	Mauritius	South Africa	Tanzania	Zimbabwe	Seychelles	DRC
SADC Founding Treaty 1992	Y	Y	Y	Y	Y	Y	Y	Y	N	N	Y	Y		N
Legal Affairs	Y	Y	Y	Y	Y	N	Y	Y	Y	N	Y	N		N
Tribunal	Y	N	Y	N	N	Y	Y	N	Y	N	N	N		N
Trade	Y	Y	Y	Y	Y	Y	N	N	Y	Y	Y	Y		N
Finance and Investment	Y	Y	N	Y	Y	Y	Y	Y	Y	Y	Y	N		N
Competition	N	N	N	N	N	N	N	N	N	N	N	N		N
Corruption	Y	Y	Y	Y	Y	Y	Y	Y	Y	Y	Y	Y		Y
Movement of Persons	Y	Y	Y	Y	N	Y	N	N	N	Y	Y	Y		N
Energy	Y	Y	Y	Y	Y	Y	Y	Y	Y	Y	Y	Y		N
Transport	Y	Y	Y	Y	Y	Y	Y	Y	Y	Y	Y	Y		N
Gender	Y	Y	Y	Y	N	Y	Y	*	*	Y		Y	Y	N
Forestry	Y	Y	Y	Y	–	–	–	Y	Y	Y	Y	Y	–	
Tourism Development	Y	Y	Y	N	Y	Y	N	Y	Y	Y	Y	Y		N
Shared Water Courses	Y	Y	Y	Y	Y	N	N	Y	N	Y	Y	Y	–	N
Mining	Y	Y	N	Y	Y	Y	N	Y	Y	Y	Y	Y		N

4.1.5 Civil society participation in the development of protocols

There are no formal processes for civil society engagement in the development of Protocols. Interested civil society organisations (CSOs) can get information directly from the relevant department of the SADC Secretariat or from the sector ministry in the member state. SADC departments also enter into partnerships with organisations offering relevant technical expertise who attend roundtables and stakeholder discussions in the development of Protocols. An example is the SADC Gender Protocol Alliance – a regional network of women's rights organisations that monitors the implementation of the Protocol in different sectors. The structure of the alliance includes lead organisations selected on the basis of technical competence in a given thematic area covered by the Protocol. Another example is the Air Pollution Information Network for Africa, a scientific network that signed a memorandum of understanding (MoU) with the SADC Environmental and Land Management Sector to participate as a stakeholder and assist in stakeholder workshops in the development of the protocol on the environment and provide technical advice for the development of the protocol article on trans-boundary air pollution.

4.1.6 The Regional Indicative Strategic Development Plan

The Regional Indicative Strategic Development Plan (RISDP) provides strategic direction in the design and formulation of SADC programmes, projects and activities from 2005 to 2015. The decision to develop the plan was made by Heads of States and Government at their 1999 Summit in Mozambique. Under the RISDP, the priority sectors for cooperation and integration are:

- Trade/economic liberalisation and development;

- Infrastructure support for regional integration;

- Sustainable food security; and

- Human and social development.

The RISDP is a plan and does not legally bind member states. However, they are expected to align their National Development Plans, frameworks, policies and strategies with the RISDP.

The goals of the RIDSP are the achievement of the following:

- A free trade area (FTA) by 2008;

- A customs union by 2010;

- A common market by 2016; and

- A monetary union by 2016.

The RIDSP also reaffirms the commitment of SADC member states to good political, economic and corporate governance, entrenched in a culture of democracy, transparency and respect for the rule of law. It promotes broad participation and consultation to engage as many stakeholders as possible, in order to create ownership for the outputs. The detailed programme can be found at www.sadc.int.

4.2 SADC organs and institutions

SADC has nine principal bodies or organs:

- Summit;

- Troika;

- Organ on Politics, Defence and Security;

- Tribunal;

- Council of Ministers;

- Integrated Committee of Ministers;

- Sectoral and Cluster Ministerial Committees;

- Standing Committee of Senior Officials;

- SADC National Committees; and

- SADC Secretariat.

In addition to the nine organs of SADC, there are a number of associated institutions, most importantly, the SADC Parliamentary Forum.

As discussed earlier, the Treaty provides in Articles 10(8), 11(3) (6) and 13(6) that the Summit and other subsidiary organs make decisions by consensus.

Figure 4.3 SADC organogram

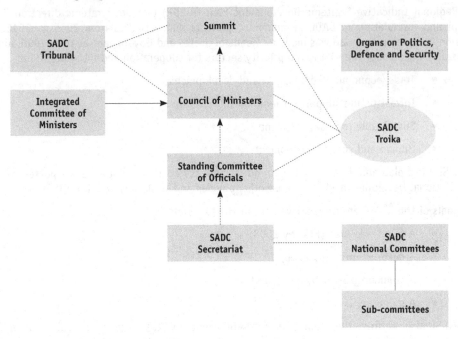

4.2.1 The Summit of Heads of State and Government

The Summit is made up of the heads of state and government of the SADC member states. It is the ultimate policy and decision-making institution of SADC and is responsible for the overall policy direction and control of functions of the Community. The Summit is a legislative organ and is capable of making decisions that are binding on all member states. Such decisions include amendments to the Treaty, Protocols, Pacts and Charters.

The decisions of the Summit are taken by consensus and this makes it susceptible to domination by larger, better-resourced member states. The Summit does not compel member states to comply with their commitments and obligations in accordance with the Treaty. It is important to note that political issues are more prominent on the Summit agenda than economic and regional integration issues. The Summit usually meets once a year in ordinary session between July and September in one of the member states. Special and extraordinary Summit meetings are also convened to discuss emergency issues when there is a need. For example, in 2009, the Summit met four times, mainly to support the transition in Zimbabwe after the Inclusive Government was set up. The host member's head of state becomes the Chair of the Summit.

The functions of the Summit are to:

- Elect a Chairperson and a Deputy Chairperson of SADC from among its members for one year on the basis of rotation;

- Select a Chairperson and a Deputy Chairperson of the SADC Organ on Politics, Defence and Security Cooperation (commonly referred to as "the Organ"), on the basis of rotation from among the members of the Summit, except that the Chairperson of the Summit cannot simultaneously be the chairperson of the Organ;

- Appoint the Executive Secretary and Deputy Secretary of the Secretariat;

- Admit new members to SADC according to Article 8 of the Treaty;

- Adopt legal instruments such as Protocols for the implementation of the provisions of the Treaty;

- Approve policy before it is considered for adoption into law, for example Protocol formulation; and

- Suspend membership of member states that contravene the Treaty.

4.2.2 The Chair and the Troika

The Chair of SADC is elected by the Summit on a rotational basis for a period of one year or from one Summit to the other. The current and immediate past and future chairs make up the Troika. The Troika was established by the Summit in Maputo, Mozambique, in 1999. According to Article 9(1) of the Treaty, the Troika applies not only to the Summit but also to the Organ, the Council, the Integrated Committee of Ministers and the Standing Committee of Officials.

According to Article 6 of the Treaty, the Troika of each institution functions as a steering committee of the institution and is, in between the meetings of the institution, responsible for:

- Decision-making;

- Facilitating the implementation of decisions; and

- Providing policy directions.

Article 9(7) gives the Troika of each institution power to create committees on an ad hoc basis.

The SADC Troika system vests authority in the three heads of state and government to take quick decisions on behalf of SADC that would ordinarily be taken at policy meetings such as the Summit or Council meetings. This also applies to the Troika of the Organ and, when combined, the two are referred to as the Double Troika.

The Troika is a key institution enabling SADC to execute tasks and implement decisions expeditiously, as well as to provide policy direction to the SADC institutions in periods between regular SADC meetings. It has proved effective in the resolution of the Zimbabwean crisis, as well as instability in the DRC and Madagascar.

4.2.3 The SADC Organ on Politics, Defence and Security Cooperation

The SADC Organ on Politics, Defence and Security Cooperation (commonly referred to as "the Organ"), is responsible for promoting peace and security in the SADC region. The Organ was established on 28 June 1996 in accordance with Article 4 of the Treaty. It is mandated to provide member states with direction regarding matters that threaten peace, security and stability in the region.

It is managed on the same Troika system as the Summit, which consists of the current, incoming and outgoing chairs, and reports to the SADC Summit Chair. The Chair of the Organ consults with the Troika of the Summit and reports to the Summit.

However, the Chairperson of the Organ cannot simultaneously hold the Chair of the Summit. Like the Summit Chair, the Organ Chair rotates on an annual basis.

The Organ promotes peace and security in the region. Its specific objectives are:

- Protecting the people and safeguarding the development of the region against instability arising from the breakdown of law and order, intra- and interstate conflict and aggression;

- Promoting political cooperation among state parties and the evolution of common political values and institutions;

- Developing common foreign policy approaches on issues of mutual concern and advancing such policy collectively in international fora;

- Promoting regional coordination and cooperation on matters relating to security and defence and establishing appropriate mechanisms to this end;

- Preventing, containing and resolving intra- and interstate conflict by peaceful means;

- Considering enforcement action in accordance with international law and as a matter of last resort where peaceful means have failed;

- Promoting the development of democratic institutions and practices within the territories of member states; and

- Encouraging the observance of universal human rights as provided for in the Charters and Conventions of the AU and UN.

The Organ has the jurisdiction to resolve conflict between state parties or between a state party and a non-state party. Examples include a conflict over territorial boundaries or natural resources, acts of aggression or other use, or threat of use, of military force and any conflict that threatens peace and security in the region.

The Organ meets more often than the Summit and its decisions and work are closely linked to the Summit. However, its resolutions can be nullified by the Summit. For example, resolutions on Zimbabwe made at the Troika Summit of the Organ held on 31 March 2011 in Livingstone, Zambia, were not endorsed by the Summit, which met the following month. The Summit merely noted the resolution, an action that did not have any legal significance.

Strategic Indicative Plan for the Organ

The Organ's mandate is operationalised through the Strategic Indicative Plan for the Organ (SIPO). The objectives of the SIPO are provided for in the Protocol on Politics, Defence and Security Cooperation and are divided into the following four thematic areas:

- *Political Sector*: Emphasises conflict prevention and management, promotion of human rights and democratic principles, promotion of peaceful coexistence, cooperation in disaster management and humanitarian assistance, and promoting a common approach to foreign policy.

- *Defence Sector*: Emphasises coordination and cooperation in matters of security, including establishing standby arrangements, joint training, the Mutual Defence Pact, developing the peacekeeping capacity of national defence forces, and coordinating the participation of state parties in international and regional peacekeeping operations.

- *State Security Sector*: Emphasises the promotion of regional coordination and cooperation in matters related to security, defence, and the prevention, containment and peaceful resolution of intra- and interstate conflicts.

- *Public Security Sector*: Emphasises cooperation between the police and state security services of member states to address cross-border crime and to promote a community-based approach to domestic security.

The Organ has two Ministerial Committees to implement the SIPO:

- The Interstate Politics and Diplomacy Committee comprises the ministers responsible for foreign affairs from each of the state parties and addresses issue of conflict prevention, management and resolution; and

- The Interstate Defence and Security Committee comprises the ministers responsible for defence, ministers responsible for public security and ministers responsible for state security from each of the state parties.

Mediation efforts by the Organ

The Organ oversees political mediation efforts in member states affected by internal conflict and other challenges. As of 2013, these countries are Lesotho, Madagascar and Zimbabwe:

- In Lesotho, the mediation efforts were formally concluded, paving the way for the general election that was held in May 2012.

- In Madagascar, the SADC facilitator, former President of Mozambique Joaquim Chissano, engaged all parties involved until a peaceful resolution to the conflict was achieved through the holding of elections. SADC established a Liaison Office in Madagascar, which was mandated with monitoring the implementation of the road map for restoring constitutional normalcy through an electoral process that was free, fair, credible and transparent. The major challenge for the SADC team was that Madagascar is a member of other regional and international networks that have launched parallel mediation efforts.

- In Zimbabwe, SADC facilitation through the President of South Africa Thabo Mbeki and later Jacob Zuma, succeeded in the three conflicting parties signing a Global Political Agreement, which resulted in the formation of the inclusive government in February 2009. The SADC facilitation team continues to engage the parties on constitutional issues and preparation for peaceful, free and fair elections.

Civil society was not directly invited to be a player in SADC-led mediation efforts in Madagascar and Zimbabwe. However, CSOs engaged with the facilitation team through briefing the South African ambassador in Harare, who also organised meetings for civil society to meet the facilitation team when it visited Harare. In addition, civil society groups held sideline meetings at the meetings of the Organ to draw attention to particular areas of the Global Political Agreement. Most of the organisations involved were human rights bodies under the umbrella of the Zimbabwe Human Rights Forum.

4.2.4 Dispute settlement mechanisms

SADC Tribunal

The SADC Tribunal was provided for under Article 16 of the 1992 Treaty and was finally implemented through a Protocol signed in 2000. The Protocol entered into force in August 2005. The Tribunal is both the judicial organ of SADC, as well as the court to settle any disputes regarding the interpretation and application of the Treaty and its Protocols. Article 14 of the Protocol of the Tribunal makes it an independent forum empowered to make rulings on the correct interpretation or application of the legal instruments of SADC. The Tribunal can make a ruling on a member state that persistently fails to fulfil the obligations of the Treaty. The Tribunal is not a Court of Appeal for SADC citizens because it was not constituted as a Regional Court of Appeal.

On 28 November 2008, the SADC Tribunal ruled that 78 white Zimbabwean farmers in *Mike Campbell (Pvt) Ltd and Others vs. Republic of Zimbabwe* could keep their farms because the Zimbabwean land reform programme had discriminated against them. The Zimbabwean government rejected this ruling, challenging its legality, and lobbied the Summit to suspend the Tribunal. The Tribunal was duly suspended by the SADC Summit held in Windhoek in August 2010, pending an independent six-month review of its "role, functions and terms of reference".

The 2011 Summit put in place a further moratorium barring the Tribunal from accepting any new cases. The Summit also paralysed the Tribunal by not renewing contracts for sitting judges or replacing them. Since they were on secondment from their member states, they went back to the benches of their respective countries. The Tribunal is unable to accept new cases since it does not comply with the requirements for its composition as prescribed by Article 3 of the SADC Tribunal Protocol, which states that the Tribunal should consist of not fewer than 10 members. The decision not to reappoint or replace the Tribunal's 10 judges has rendered the Tribunal inoperative since August 2012. The Tribunal has only four remaining judges.

In addition, its mandate has been revised to make the Tribunal an arbiter on matters relating to the implementation of SADC Protocols. It is envisaged that it will interpret the Treaty for the benefit of member states in an advisory capacity only. When it arbitrates on Protocols, its decisions should become legally binding. Due to the fact that Article 4 of the Treaty has not been translated into a Protocol on Human Rights, for the time being it will only hear cases arising among the member states. The implication is that aggrieved individuals (natural and juristic persons) cannot take a member state to the Tribunal. Some member states have expressed the view that excluding citizen participation in dispute settlement at the SADC level could force them to explore dispute settlement mechanisms outside the continent, such as the International Court of Justice, a costly process.

CSO reactions to SADC Tribunal suspension

International Commission of Jurists, Southern Africa Litigation Centre, SADC Lawyers Association to Ministers of Justice on the SADC Tribunal, June 2012

The decision by the Summit rendered the Tribunal inoperative.

It was taken without adequate consultation with and participation of civil society, the SADC Parliamentary Forum or Pan African Parliament.

The group advocated preservation of access by private persons to the SADC Tribunal as this was consistent with international standards and practice. They argued that the Treaty establishing the African Economic Community (AEC) seeks to coordinate and harmonise the policies of the AU and its regional economic communities. The decision to limit, restrict or block access by private persons to the SADC Tribunal contradicts the Treaty establishing the AEC and seriously undermines the rule of law in southern Africa.

'What makes matters worse is the apparent lack of respect for the rule of law by the member-state governments, as exemplified by their disabling of the SADC Tribunal, which makes it impossible to operationalise rule-based governance.' Association of SADC Business Councils and Chambers of Industry.

Trade Panel

The Trade Protocol adopted in 1996 provided in its Annex VI for the establishment of a Trade Panel, modelled on the World Trade Organisation dispute-settlement mechanism. The Trade Panel's jurisdiction is limited to interstate trade disputes. Unlike the Tribunal, which was designed as a permanent institution, the Protocol's Dispute Settlement Mechanism is an ad hoc institution. That means the body deciding a particular dispute is composed of panellists nominated and selected for a particular dispute only. So far no cases have been brought before the Trade Panel.

4.2.5 Council of Ministers

The Council of Ministers is composed of Ministers of Foreign Affairs, Economic Planning and Finance. It is dominated by the Ministers of Foreign Affairs, who play the leading role in facilitating these meetings. The Council is chaired by the minister of the hosting government (from the same country as the Chair of the Summit).

The responsibilities of the Council of Ministers are outlined in the Treaty. They include:

- Overseeing the implementation of the policies of SADC and the proper execution of its programmes;
- Advising the Summit on matters of overall policy and efficient and harmonious functioning and development of SADC, including the establishment of directorates, committees, other institutions and organs;
- Directing, coordinating and supervising the operations of the institutions of SADC subordinate to it;
- Recommending to the Summit persons for appointment to the posts of Executive Secretary and Deputy Executive Secretary;
- Developing and implementing the SADC Common Agenda and strategic priorities; and
- Convening conferences and other meetings as appropriate for purposes of promoting the objectives and programmes of SADC.

Under the new structure adopted in 2001, it was recommended that the Council meet four times a year to facilitate speedy decision-making and to allow more time to discuss regional issues and take stock of progress in the RIDSP. The Council is the direct link between SADC and member states and the ministers are mandated to express member states' policy positions on regional matters.

The Council plays an important role in advising the Summit on matters of overall policy and the efficient and harmonious functioning and development of SADC. Since the Summit meets once a year in ordinary session, this role is critical in keeping the heads of state and government informed of developments on SADC issues. The Council also raises awareness by convening conferences and other meetings to promote objectives and programmes critical for regional integration. It is instrumental in making recommendations on new members who wish to join the SADC. It therefore directly influences the process of regional integration. A major weakness is that the SADC Council of Ministers, unlike that of the AU, has no decision-making powers. It can only make recommendations to the Summit.

Table 4.5 Agenda template for the Council of Ministers

1	Adoption of agenda
2	Annual member states contributions
3	Report of the Executive Secretary
4	Review of the implementation of Council decisions
5	Report of the Ministerial Troika
6	Report of the Finance Committee
7	Report of the Audit Committee
8	Reports of Sectoral and Cluster Ministerial Meetings
9	Legal issues
10	Items proposed by member states for consideration
11	Summit agenda
12	Any other business

Civil society influence

Unlike UN and AU meetings, where the agenda is posted on the website, the agenda and papers for the SADC Summit and Council of Ministers meetings are not available before the meeting. Civil society has to rely on national governments and/or Secretariat officials for information on the key agenda items. This undermines preparations by CSOs, who often have to rely on the theme for guidance on issues of priority. They are unable to influence the agenda on issues such as human rights, civic participation and social dialogue. There is also no channel to provide technical inputs to the Summit or Council of Ministers by CSOs. Publications and communiqués from civil society are widely circulated during Summits and the preceding Council of Ministers meetings without a formal channel for making input. Ministers from member states, as well as senior officials from the Secretariat, accept invitations to CSO sideline meetings and events where they are handed communiqués and statements for onward transmission. There is thus no platform to distil best practices, share and learn from each other at the SADC level. Outside the Summit, civil society can influence the technical departments of the SADC Secretariat.

4.2.6 The Integrated Committee of Ministers

The Integrated Committee of Ministers (ICM) was one of the new institutions established in the restructuring of SADC in 2001 to ensure the smooth implementation of regional programmes and projects. However, a review of the decision-making process found that the ICM was not adding value but duplicating the Council of Ministers' role. In November 2007, the Council, after wide consultations, abolished the ICM. It was replaced by the Sectoral and Cluster Ministerial Committees.

4.2.7 Sectoral and Cluster Ministerial Committees

The Sectoral and Cluster Ministerial Committees comprise ministers from each SADC member state, grouped by thematic responsibility; each has a mandate to meet at least once a year. This system is aimed at ensuring proper policy guidance, coordination and harmonisation of cross-sectoral activities.

There are six Cluster Committees that consist of ministers responsible for:

- Trade, industry, finance and investment;

- Infrastructure and services;

- Food, agriculture, natural resources and the environment;

- Social and human development and special programmes (HIV/AIDS, education, labour, employment and gender);

- Politics, defence and security; and

- Legal affairs and judicial matters.

4.2.8 Standing Committee of Senior Officials

The Standing Committee of Senior Officials is a technical advisory committee to the Council of Ministers. It meets at least four times a year in preparation for meetings of the Council of Ministers. It consists of one senior official, usually a permanent or principal secretary or an official of equivalent rank from each member state, generally from the same ministry as the minister who sits in the Council of Ministers. The Chairperson and Vice-Chairperson of the Standing Committee are appointed from the same member states as the Chair and Vice-Chair of the Council.

The Standing Committee is strategic in channelling information from SADC to the member states' National Contact Points. This promotes awareness about economic integration among the member states. Its frequent meetings can serve as an expediting tool for the SADC regional economic integration agenda. It also processes documentation from the ICM and reports to the Council.

4.2.9 SADC National Committees

The Treaty makes specific provision for a participatory process that 'encourages the peoples of the region and their institutions to take initiatives to develop economic, social and cultural ties across the region and to participate fully in the implementation of the programmes and projects of SADC.' In 2001, the Treaty was amended to provide for the formation of SADC National Committees (SNCs), composed of government, labour and CSOs at member-state level. The SNCs were conceived as a channel by which institutions and stakeholders at national level could provide input and guidance to SADC in the formulation of regional policies and strategies, as well as a platform for coordinating and overseeing the implementation of programmes at the national level. SNC decisions can be overridden by the Council of Ministers, which takes decisions at intergovernmental level without consulting the SNCs. This has implications for the ownership of SADC initiatives, especially where regional integration lacks popular support and the participation of citizens of member states. SNCs can also initiate SADC projects and prepare issue papers as an input into the preparation of regional strategies. SNCs have a direct link with the Secretariat and have an input into regional policy formulation.

SNCs consist of key stakeholders from government, the private sector and civil society in each member state. Depending on the member state, the Secretariats of the SNCs are located in the ministry responsible for SADC matters, usually the Ministry of Foreign Affairs, Ministry of Trade, Ministry of Finance or Ministry of Economic Planning. SNC meetings are generally held on an ad hoc basis as they prepare for Council and Summit Meetings and disseminate information on SADC programmes.

According to Article 16A of the Treaty, the functionality of an SNC is assessed in terms of its having an established Secretariat, stakeholder participation, financing by member states, structures and meetings. Some 12 years after the initiation of the SNCs, only Botswana, Mozambique and Mauritius are perceived to have fully functional Committees. In other member states, the SNCs either exist only on paper or do not exist at all.

> **The SADC National Commission in Mozambique**
>
> The structure of the SNC in Mozambique (CONSADC) is as follows:
> - Chairperson;
> - Plenary;
> - Ministerial cluster groups;
> - Technical cluster groups;
> - Provincial contact points;
> - Secretariat; and
> - Secretariat Advisory Committee.
>
> The Chairperson of CONSADC is the Minister of Foreign Affairs and Cooperation.
>
> **Plenary**
>
> The Plenary is the highest body in the hierarchy of CONSADC and meets at least once a year. It consists of all Cabinet ministers and chief executives of NGOs and CSOs, trade unions, private sector and other associations.
>
> **Ministerial cluster groups**
>
> The following ministerial cluster groups are included:
> - Trade, Industry, Finance and Investment Cluster;
> - Food, Agriculture and Natural Resources Cluster;
> - Infrastructure and Services Cluster; and
> - Social and Human Resources Development Cluster.
>
> **Technical cluster groups**
>
> Technical cluster groups meet once a month and are made up of a smaller number of members with the same composition of government and civil society.
>
> **Provincial contact points**
>
> Each province has a contact point appointed by the governor, usually a provincial director for one of the cluster ministries.
>
> **Secretariat**
>
> The Secretariat has fully dedicated premises and is funded through the state budget. Its structure is as follows:
> - One Director;
> - One Deputy Director;
> - Three departments: Planning, Documentation, Administration and Finance;
> - Four technical staff members: Planning Department, Documentation Department and heads of sections of Human Resources and Finances; and
> - Seven support staff members.
>
> The Secretariat services the clusters and assists the provinces.
>
> **Secretariat Advisory Committee**
>
> The Secretariat has an Advisory Committee that meets once a month and is chaired by the CONSADC Director. Its composition is as follows:
> - CONSADC Director;
> - CONSADC Deputy Director;
> - Heads of CONSADC departments (three in total); and
> - Coordinators of the technical clusters from the Ministries of Health, Agriculture, Finance and Transport, and Communications.

4.2.10 The SADC Secretariat

The Secretariat is the principal executive institution of SADC and has its headquarters in Gaborone, Botswana. It is headed by an Executive Secretary, who is appointed by the Summit for a period of four years, renewable. The main functions of the Secretariat according to Article 14 of the Treaty are:

- Strategic planning and management of SADC programmes;
- Implementation of the decisions of the Summit and Council;
- Organisation and management of SADC meetings;
- Financial and general administration;
- Representation and promotion of SADC; and
- Promotion and harmonisation of policies and strategies of member states.

In addition, the Secretariat performs the following functions:

- Gender mainstreaming in all SADC programmes and activities;
- Organising and managing the meetings of the Troika and any other committees established by the Summit, Council and the Troika on an ad hoc basis;
- Submitting harmonised policies and programmes to the Council for consideration and approval;
- Monitoring and evaluating the implementation of regional policies and programmes;
- Collating and disseminating information on the Community and maintaining a reliable database;
- Developing capacity, infrastructure and maintenance of an intraregional ICT platform;
- Mobilising resources, coordinating and harmonising programmes and projects with cooperating partners;
- Devising appropriate strategies for self-financing and income-generating activities and investment;
- Managing special programmes and projects; and
- Undertaking research on community-building and the integration process.

The Secretariat has the following eight Directorates:

- The Organ on Politics, Defence and Security Cooperation;
- Trade, Industry, Finance and Investment;
- Infrastructure and Services;
- Food, Agriculture and Natural Resources;
- Social and Human Development and Special Programmes;
- Policy, Planning and Resource Mobilisation;
- Budget and Finance; and
- Human Resources and Administration.

There are also five standalone units responsible for cross-cutting issues established by the Council of Ministers under Article 15(4) and (5) of the Treaty:

- Internal Audit;
- Information and Communications Technology;
- Gender and Development;
- Legal Affairs; and
- Public Relations.

Figure 4.4 Structure of the Secretariat

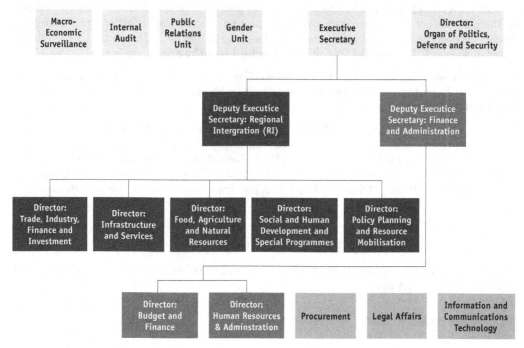

4.2.11 The SADC Parliamentary Forum

The SADC Parliamentary Forum (SADC-PF) is an initiative of the parliaments in SADC. It is a regional body composed of Members of Parliament (MPs) from the national parliaments of SADC member states. It represents over 3,500 MPs from the SADC region. The SADC-PF is a regional organisation in its own right but remains linked to SADC. Established in 1996, it was approved by the Summit in 1997 as an autonomous institution of SADC, in accordance with Article 9(2) of the Treaty. It therefore has no reporting relationship with the Summit

The SADC-PF consists of Presiding Officers and four representatives elected by the national Parliament of each member state and reflecting its gender and political composition, in line with the constitution of the Forum. The specific objectives of the SADC-PF are to address a wide range of issues, including, but not limited to, the following:

- Promotion of human rights, gender equality, good governance, democracy and transparency;

- Promotion of peace, security and stability;

- Hastening the pace of economic cooperation, development and integration on the basis of equity and mutual benefits;

- Facilitating networking with other interparliamentary organisations;

- Promoting the participation of NGOs, business and intellectual communities in SADC activities;

- Familiarising the peoples of SADC with the aims and objectives of SADC; and

- Informing SADC of the popular views on development and issues affecting the region.

It is important to note that the Summit has not endorsed the SADC-PF as a regional parliament, so it is unable to meaningfully promote civic participation and influence policy formulation. Thus, it does not have a reporting relationship with the Summit and other SADC institutions, but works together with them on matters of common interest. It strives to involve people and political parties in SADC in the regional integration process.

The Plenary Assembly is the main policy-making and deliberative organ where all 15 national parliaments of SADC are represented. It meets twice a year to make policy decisions and forward recommendations to the SADC Summit of Heads of State and Government on various issues affecting the SADC region. Plenary Assembly decisions are implemented by an Executive Committee and supported by a Secretariat based in Windhoek, Namibia. The SADC-PF Secretariat is headed by a Secretary-General.

The SADC-PF sends representatives to observe elections in SADC member states, attends Council meetings and collaborates with the SADC Secretariat on harmonisation of policies and regulatory frameworks concerning HIV/AIDS matters.

There has been debate within SADC-PF that it should become an organ of SADC with legislative and oversight powers, as is the case in the East African Community. The proposal was rejected. In response, SADC-PF came up with a Draft Protocol on the SADC Parliament. At its meeting in Luanda in 2011, the Council of Ministers recommended that the SADC Heads of State and Government (Summit) continue to encourage the activities of SADC-PF, but not support the establishment of the SADC Parliament.

4.3 The decision-making process in SADC

Figure 4.5 is an illustration of the decision-making structures of SADC, which are discussed in more detail on the following pages.

Figure 4.5 The decision-making structures of SADC

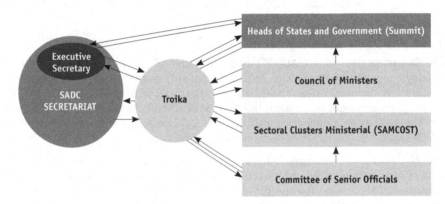

4.3.1 The Summit

The Summit of Heads of State and Government is SADC's supreme policy-making institution. It provides overall policy direction and control of the organisation and its various institutions and functions including the RIDSP, adopting and amending SADC Treaties, as well as appointing the Executive Secretary and the judges of the Tribunal. The Summit is therefore the most important decision-making body of SADC as it has to approve policies before they are adopted into law, for example, as Protocols. Even the judgments of the SADC Tribunal have to be referred to the Summit, since it is the only body that can sanction the findings of the Tribunal.

The fact that all decisions are taken at the Summit has caused some key stakeholders to express concern that issues become diluted as they go up the decision-making ladder. In addition, the perennial political problems faced in the region have resulted in SADC being seen as a political body in which economic issues have been sidelined.

The decisions of the Summit are made by consensus. However, there are some exceptions to the consensus rule. For example, three quarters of all members have to approve an amendment to the SADC Treaty for it to be passed. Decisions regarding admission of new members are based on unanimity.

The SADC Treaty is silent on whether the binding decisions of the Summit have a direct effect on the laws of member states. In addition, SADC has no mechanisms to follow up implementation of the decisions of the Summit by member states, making implementation discretionary.

Special Summit meetings are called to discuss emergency issues. These are in most cases political. For example, the SADC heads held an extraordinary summit in the wings of the 2014 AU Summit to approve the elections in Madagascar and to remove all sanctions placed on the country.

SADC is a very political organisation with powers resting in member governments and especially heads of state. The organisation's character is also influenced by the character and personality of the head of state who chairs the institution.

CSOs can engage ministers and officials from the country of the Chair even outside the Summit. This has become common in cases of political issues; for example, civil society groups from Zimbabwe, Madagascar, DRC and Swaziland, have held meetings in the country of the Chair and sought meetings with senior officials from the country.

Civil society wishing to influence the Summit can do so through representatives of the member governments. Often, influence at the level of the Summit is possible on political issues but not on issues covered by the RIDSP. For these, it is more effective to influence decision-making at the lower levels.

Unlike those of the AU and other RECs, the agenda and papers of the SADC Summit are not made public. This makes it difficult to influence the decisions of the institution. For example, in 2013, there was an SADC extraordinary summit at which most CSOs expected the issue of Zimbabwe to be discussed. A great deal of resources were deployed in getting civil society to Addis Ababa and in preparing dossiers. The Summit dwelt on Madagascar and the DRC with only a passing reference to Zimbabwe. The official word was that Zimbabwe was not even on the agenda.

4.3.2 The Troika

According to Article 9(1) of the Treaty, the Troika structure applies to the Summit, Organ, Council, Integrated Committee of Ministers and Standing Committee of Officials. The Troika of each institution functions as a steering committee and is responsible for decision-making, facilitating the implementation of decisions, and providing policy direction. Both the SADC Troika and Troika of the Organ on Politics, Defence and Security Cooperation are empowered to take quick decisions on behalf of SADC, which would ordinarily be taken at the Summit or Council meetings. When the Troikas of the Organ and the Summit meet, the meeting is referred to as a Double Troika meeting. This becomes a powerful meeting whose decisions carry much weight, as it comprises six heads of state. The Double Troika has met to deliberate on political matters such as crises in member states, as well as on economic cooperation with strategic partners of SADC such as the EU.

Troikas provide policy direction to the SADC institutions and make quick decisions in periods between regular SADC meetings. The decisions will still need to be put before the Summit, which can endorse, nullify or note them. For example, resolutions on Zimbabwe made at the Troika Summit of the Organ on Politics, Defence and Security held in Livingstone, Zambia, were not endorsed by the Summit that met the following month. The Summit merely noted the resolution – a move that did not convey any legal significance.

4.3.3 The Council of Ministers

The Council of Ministers advises the Summit on matters of overall policy and any others matters that affect the harmonious functioning and development of SADC. It oversees the functioning of SADC, the implementation of policies and the execution of programmes, including the RISDP and SIPO. It develops the agenda for the Summit and during the annual Summit, makes decisions and recommendations to be endorsed by the Summit. Decisions include issues of member-state contributions and the implementation of the RIDSP.

The Council is therefore the most influential body in the decision-making processes of SADC. It influences almost all the decisions made by the heads of state. Civil society wishing to influence SADC decisions can do so by influencing the ministers who sit on the Council. They are mostly Ministers of Foreign Affairs or ministers responsible for international cooperation. The challenge for civil society is that the Ministry of Foreign Affairs is not very approachable even in the home country. However, each country has a SADC desk and contact point, often in the Ministry of Foreign Affairs, with which civil society can engage. Depending on the decision, an organisation that wishes to influence it may find it more effective to engage the sectoral ministries in member countries.

4.3.4 Standing Committee of Officials

The decisions and recommendations of the Council of Ministers originate from the Standing Committee of Officials, which therefore provides another point of influence for civil society.

It is important to be aware of progress on the issues you wish to influence so as to provide relevant input to the Standing Committee. The SADC Secretariat or the respective technical ministry in the member state are the best source of information. Influence is through advocacy and bilateral engagement with specific country officials, especially the Chair. There is no formal provision for participation of non-state actors in these meetings.

4.3.5 Sectoral and Cluster Ministerial Committees

The Sectoral and Cluster Ministerial Committees (SAMCOST) have an oversight role over the activities of the core areas of integration, monitor and control the implementation of the RISDP in their area of competence, and provide policy advice and recommendations to the Council of Ministers and the Directorates of the Secretariat. The only decisions made in these fora are technical, relating to which recommendations are forwarded to the Council of Ministers.

SAMCOST provides the best opportunity for civil society to influence SADC processes and decisions. Civil society wishing to influence this forum can do so as experts invited by the Secretariat for the different sectoral meetings, where they can present papers and influence recommendations. This requires building relationships with the different divisions of the Secretariat.

4.3.6 The Secretariat

The Secretariat is SADC's principal administrative and executive institution. Among its chief tasks are strategic planning and policy analysis, monitoring, coordinating and supporting the implementation of SADC programmes, implementation of decisions of supreme decision-making bodies and Troikas and representation and promotion of SADC. The Executive Secretary makes decisions on operational matters.

A recent midterm review of the RIDSP concluded that SADC is a government-centred as opposed to a people-centred organisation. The mechanisms for non-state-actor participation mechanisms such as the SADC National Councils are not well developed. SADC has limited its MoUs with civil society to the labour umbrella organisation, the faith-based organisation umbrella and the NGO umbrella. Influencing SADC is therefore an opportunistic process requiring familiarity with the technical areas of the RISDP, centred on forming relations with the Directorates so as to be considered a technical partner. Technical partners can present technical papers to SAMCOST and influence its recommendations.

There is no clear route for civil society wishing to influence SADC on political issues. The best route is through the Chair of SADC and the Organ as well as other members of the two Troikas.

4.4 Budgets and financing of SADC activities

Every three years the Secretariat prepares a Budget Outlook Paper (BOP) to ensure that there is balance between financial resources and the priorities set by both the RISDP and SIPO. Drawing from the BOP, the Secretariat prepares a corporate plan as well as a business plan on an annual basis.

4.4.1 The SADC budget

The resources for the SADC Programme of Action are determined and provided in accordance with Article 9 of the Treaty. This provision states that funds can be provided by member states and the International Cooperating Partners (ICPs).

According to the RISDP, SADC's financing requirements can be divided into financing for SADC's coordination function and financing for development activities. SADC's coordination function is financed mainly through membership contributions and is based on the proportional contribution of each member state to the combined SADC GDP. Member states also implement SADC projects at national level.

For example, the SADC Council, at its March 2010 meeting in Windhoek, Namibia, approved estimates of expenditure for 2011/2012 of USD 83.6 million to be funded by member-state contributions and the ICPs as outlined in Table 4.6. (The 2010/2011 budget was USD 77.8 million and actual spending USD 59.0 million.)

Table 4.6 The 2011/2012 Budget (USD million)

Source of funding	2010/2011 Budget	2010/2011 Actual	2011/2012 Budget	Change % against actual
Annual member states' contributions	26.039	26.551	31.500	19%
Accumulated funds	1.800	1.800	0	-100%
Member states' HIV/AIDS contributions	3.025	0.512	0	-100%
Subtotal	30.864	28.863	31.500	9%
ICPs	46.434	29.390	51.500	75%
Other sources	0.780	0.745	0.586	-21%
Repayment to reserves	-0.300	0	0	
Total	77.778	58.998	83.586	42%

Source: SADC Secretariat: Budget for the year ending 31 March 2012

Table 4.7 Analysis of approved 2011/2012 budget per intervention area

Business areas	Contracted discretionary and statutory expenditure		Direct programme expenditure		Total	
	Amount (USD million)	Proportion (%)	Amount	Proportion (%)	Amount	Proportion (%)
Organ for Politics, Defence and Security Cooperation	1.698	7%	1.297	17%	2.995	9%
Trade, industry, finance and investment	1.927	8%	0.907	12%	2.835	9%
Infrastructure and services	1.315	5%	0.739	10%	2.054	6%
Food, agriculture and natural resources	1.395	6%	1.351	18%	2.747	9%
Social, human development and special projects	0.915	4%	2.490	33%	3.406	11%
Policy planning and resource mobilisation	1.165	5%	0.429	6%	1.594	5%
Macro-economic surveillance	0.122	0%	0.25	0%	0.147	0%
Gender	0.260	1%	0.120	2%	0.380	1%
SADC Tribunal	1.122	5%	0.138	2%	1.260	4%
Corporate services	10.107	41%	–	0%	10.107	32%
SADC House Unitary Charges	4.524	18%	–	0%	4.524	14%
Total	24.551	100%	7.498	100%	32.049	100%
Proportion	77%		23%		100%	

4.4.2 Annual member states' contributions

The funds due from member states as contributions in 2011/2012 were determined in accordance with the approved formula (Table 4.8).

Table 4.8 Status of annual member states' contributions as at 30 September 2011 (USD million)

Balance	Approved amount	Received	Balance
Angola	3.210	3.210	–
Botswana	1.943	1.943	–
DRC	1.881	1.881	–
Lesotho	1.622	1.622	–
Madagascar	1.789	–	1.789
Malawi	1.677	1.677	–
Mauritius	1.825	1.825	–
Mozambique	1.833	1.833	–
Namibia	1.841	1.841	–
Seychelles	0.121	0.121	–
South Africa	6.268	5.868	0.400
Swaziland	1.660	1.388	0.272
Tanzania	2.122	1.759	0.363
Zambia	1.913	1.913	–
Zimbabwe	1.757	1.757	–
SADC TOTAL	31.462	28.638	2.824

Source: SADC Secretariat: Management Accounts for the period to 30 September 2011

Sanctions against member states in arrears

According to Article 33 of the Treaty, sanctions can be imposed against a member state that is in arrears. The Council of Ministers decided to impose the sanctions as follows:

- When in arrears for one year, suspension of the member state's right to speak and receive documentation at meetings of SADC.

- When in arrears for two years, suspension of:

  - The member state's right to speak and receive documentation at meetings of SADC; and

  - Recruitment and renewal of contracts of employment of personnel from the member state by SADC.

- When in arrears for three years, suspension of:

  - The member state's right to speak and receive documentation at meetings of SADC;

  - Recruitment and renewal of contracts of employment of personnel from the member state by SADC; and

  - Provision by SADC of funds for new projects in the member state.

- When in arrears for four or more years, suspension of:

  - The member state's right to speak and receive documentation at meetings of SADC;

  - Recruitment and renewal of contracts of employment of personnel from the member state by SADC;

- Provision by SADC of funds for new projects in the member state; and

- Cooperation between SADC and the member state in the areas of cooperation.

The Seychelles is the only country that has resigned from SADC due to an inability to pay its member-state contributions. The country withdrew from SADC in July 2003, but this only became effective in July 2004. Seychelles Ministry of Foreign Affairs officials said at the time that there was little justification for the money Seychelles was expected to contribute to the regional organisation annually, especially at a time when it was undergoing difficulties with a shortage of foreign exchange. The country rejoined SADC in 2008.

4.4.3 International Cooperating Partners

The ICPs contribute to the SADC Secretariat's operational budget and to the bulk of the projects in the form of grants and financing agreements through different mechanisms and procedures. SADC's main cooperating partners are the European Union (EU), the African Development Bank (AfDB), the World Bank, the Commonwealth, the World Health Organisation, the Food and Agriculture Organisation and the Global Fund to Fight AIDS, Tuberculosis and Malaria. Regional institutions such as the Forum for Agricultural Research in Africa and the Southern African Trust also support SADC technically and financially. The bilateral donors include Germany, France, Norway, Sweden and the United Kingdom.

The predominance of ICP funds in SADC budgets has been described as unsustainable. The Executive Secretary in his report to the Council of Ministers for 2011/2012 outlined the problem, saying the current funding mechanism comprising funds from member states and development partners does not allow for movement of funds between actions funded by either source. The funding required from member states to support the staff establishment required to implement approved programmes is above the current financial contributions. As a result, there is low absorption capacity for donor funds. In a statement to commemorate World AIDS Day the Executive Secretary said that "Studies have shown that over 82% of the AIDS response in the SADC region is financed from external resources. This situation is unacceptable and we need to take decisive and concrete steps to reverse it."

Table 4.9 SADC ICP by thematic areas

Thematic Group	SADC Focal Point	ICP Focal Point
1. Water sector	Infrastructure and Services Directorate	Germany
2. Transport	Infrastructure and Services Directorate	DfID (UK)
3. Energy	Infrastructure and Services Directorate	Norway
4. HIV/AIDS	Social and Human Development and Special Programmes Directorate	Sweden
5. Agriculture and food security	Food, Agriculture and Natural Resources Directorate	DfID
6. Natural resources	Food, Agriculture and Natural Resources Directorate	FAO
7. Trade facilitation	Trade, Industry, Finance and Investment Directorate	EU
8. Peace and security	Organ on Politics, Defence and Security	Austria

Table 4.10 Comparative contributions by member states and ICPs to the SADC budget (USD million)

Source	Budget 2011/2012	Budget 2010/2011	Actual
Member states' contributions	31.5	30.864	28.86
Development partners	51.5	46.434	29.39

Source: SADC 2011

Civil society and other analysts have called on member states to address this problem, which is exacerbated by the non-participatory nature of SADC, whereby member-state governments dominate at the expense of key stakeholders such as national legislatures, CSOs and the business community. By virtue of their financial contributions and technical expertise, ICPs have more access to information about SADC and have a greater influence on it than citizens. Chairperson Namibian President Hifikepunye Pohamba's report for the period covering August 2010 to July 2011 called for reducing external funding by increasing the member states' contributions, as well as accountability and operational efficiency.

4.5 Relationship with the AU

One of the objectives of the AU, as contained in the Constitutive Act, is to coordinate and harmonise policies between the existing and future RECs for the gradual attainment of the objectives of the Union. SADC is one of five RECs recognised by the AU as building blocks to integration. The AU has come up with a Minimum Integration Programme (MIP) for 2009–2012. The MIP breaks down the Abuja Treaty into priority programmes and projects in key sectors.

In its 2011–2012 report to the Council of Ministers, the SADC Secretariat reported that it continued to implement most activities in the AU MIP. According to the SADC Secretariat, the RISDP and SIPO, which are the basis for SADC's medium-term and short-term plans, are much more comprehensive integration agendas than the MIP.

The SADC Secretariat attends the regular AU Summits, including the January and July Executive Council and Assembly Meetings as well as the annual meetings of the AU Commission, RECs and strategic partners. The country holding the Chair of SADC also organises caucuses at ambassadorial, ministerial and heads of state and government levels at the AU so as to agree common positions.

SADC and the AU have worked closely in areas of peace and security. For example, on the Zimbabwe crisis, the AU deferred to the SADC Organ to advise it on developments and recommend actions. SADC and the Peace and Security Council of the AU have also worked together on the conflicts in the DRC and Madagascar.

The SADC Secretariat plays an active role in assisting SADC member states in their quest for the positions of Chairperson of the AU Commission and key Commissioners. SADC successfully lobbied to get Nkosazana Dlamini-Zuma elected to the post of Chairperson of the AU Commission. She was presented as the SADC rather than the South African candidate, giving her candidacy weight. SADC sent campaign teams made up of foreign ministers of the Double Troika plus Zimbabwe to visit key African governments and has proved itself to be a strong political force at the AU.

4.5.1 Africa Standby Force

The Africa Standby Force was established by the AU in 2004 as an international, continental African military force, with both a civilian and police component, under the direction of the AU. Each of the RECs agreed to provide a brigade. The SADC Brigade was officially launched in August 2007. It was part of the AU deployments in Sudan. The Brigade's operations centre is in Gaborone, Botswana, as part of the SADC Secretariat.

4.5.2 The New Partnership for Africa's Development

The mandates of SADC and the goals of its RISDP are closely linked to the mandate and priorities of the New Partnership for Africa's Development (NEPAD). The NEPAD programme is supported by the Heads of State and Government Orientation Committee, which includes 20 member states. Five of these member states are from the SADC region, namely South Africa, Namibia, Lesotho, Malawi and the DRC. South Africa is a major sponsor of NEPAD and has hosted the Secretariat since its establishment. In addition, President Jacob Zuma of South Africa is championing the Continental Infrastructure Development initiative, which is proving instrumental in stepping up an integrated programme of infrastructure development across the continent, in line with the Programme for Infrastructure Development in Africa.

4.5.3 Peace, security and elections

The generally accepted minimum conditions for holding free and fair elections in SADC are derived from two principal frameworks. These are the *SADC Principles and Guidelines for Holding Elections* and the *African Charter on Democracy, Elections and Governance*. Article 2 of the SADC Principles of 2004 provides for:

- Full participation of citizens in the political process;

- Freedom of association;

- Political tolerance;

- Regular intervals for elections as provided for by the respective national constitutions;

- Equal opportunity for all political parties to access the state media;

- Equal opportunity to exercise the right to vote and be voted for;

- Independence of the judiciary and impartiality of electoral institutions;

- Voter education;

- Acceptance of the election results by political parties; and

- The election proclaimed to have been free and fair by the competent national electoral authorities in accordance with the law of the land.

SADC concluded two mediation efforts in Zimbabwe and Madagascar, discussed in more detail in 4.3.2 above (Mediation Efforts by the Organ).

4.6 Civil society in SADC

4.6.1 Treaty provisions

The preamble to the Treaty provides that:

- SADC shall seek to involve fully the people of the region and key stakeholders in the process of regional integration. SADC shall cooperate with and support the initiatives of the peoples of the region and key stakeholders, contributing to the objectives of this Treaty in the areas of cooperation in order to foster closer relations among the communities, associations and people of the region.

The key stakeholders are defined to include the private sector, NGOs and workers' and employer organisations. Article 23 of the Treaty provides for participation of stakeholders in SADC through the SADC National Committees. Stakeholder participation is also referred to in the RIDSP and SIPO.

According to the Council of Ministers, there has been extensive collaboration between SADC and the key stakeholders, which has facilitated their participation in the following:

- Policy-making and technical meetings;

- Consultative conferences;

- The International Conference on Poverty and Development;

- Negotiations on the SADC Free Trade Area;

- The launch of the Free Trade Area; and

- The development and adoption of the Protocol on Gender and Development.

In 2011, the Council of Ministers reaffirmed its decision that key stakeholders should participate in the SADC integration agenda through the SADC National Committees. This appears to block off direct participation at regional level, with the exception of existing arrangements with organisations (for example, MoUs). However, CSOs can work directly at the technical level with departments. A successful example is the work on the SADC Gender Protocol, which involved ministers responsible for gender issues, civil society and the Secretariat in first its development and now in its implementation through the SADC Protocol Alliance. The Southern Africa Trust also works with the SADC Secretariat on the Poverty Observatory Initiative and has seconded a policy adviser to the SADC Secretariat to advise on poverty reduction.

Civil society has expressed concern that SADC continues to be a political entity overly focused on heads of state at the expense of an open and participatory process. At their meeting on the sidelines of the 2007 Summit, CSOs expressed concern at the lack of commitment by SADC member states to the domestication of regional Declarations and Protocols. They were also concerned by the non-adherence to Protocols and Declarations by some member states, many instances resulting in internal conflicts and instability, which slowed down or reversed the agenda of regional integration. Examples provided included the SADC election guidelines listed in 4.5.3 above. They recommended that the Heads of State and Government:

- Adopt and develop concrete national and regional implementation strategies for the Protocol on Gender and Development and other strategic declarations enhancing development of the region; and

- Provide concrete mechanisms of checks and balances among themselves as peers in order to ensure accountability and enforcement of the protocols agreed upon.

SADC appears to have bowed to the pressure from civil society and is undertaking a programme to operationalise Article 23 of the SADC Treaty on stakeholder participation.

4.6.2 Regional civil society networks with memoranda of understanding with SADC

The SADC Secretariat has signed MoUs with some regional civil society networks, among them the Southern African Trade Union Coordination Council, the Association of SADC Chambers of Commerce and Industry, the SADC Council of Non-Governmental Organisations, and the Forum for Former Heads of State and Government. These MoUs provide a legal framework for cooperation and collaboration between SADC and key stakeholders in working towards the common goals of sustainable development, economic growth and poverty alleviation. The organisations with MoUs are also referred to as apex bodies, as they are seen to represent clusters of stakeholders. Such MoUs have to be approved by the Council of Ministers, implying a long drawn-out process, often taking years to conclude. A number of regional organisations have become frustrated at going back and forth in pursuit of MoUs. For example, the Food, Agriculture and Natural Recourses Policy Analysis Network, a key partner for SADC in the implementation of the RIDSP since 1994, has not yet succeeded in signing an MoU with the SADC Secretariat.

The Southern African Trade Union Coordination Council

The aim of the Southern African Trade Union Coordination Council (SATUCC) is to unite working people and the poor and voiceless in the struggle to free southern Africa from exploitation, injustice and oppression by providing a dynamic, inclusive and sustainable platform to influence regional policy in favour of the working populations and the poor. Its objectives include:

- Building a democratic and independent trade union movement in southern Africa;

- Promoting and defending human and trade union rights as well as fundamental freedoms as enshrined in the Treaty, Charters and Protocols, the African Charter on Human and Peoples' Rights, The International Labour Organisation (ILO) Declaration on Fundamental Principles and Rights at Work and its Follow-up, and the UN Universal Declaration of Human Rights; and

- Engaging with SADC's development and integration agenda in a manner that protects and advances interests of the working class and the wider society, especially vulnerable sectors like women, migrants, elderly, children, the unemployed and workers in the informal economy.

SATUCC has worked with the Secretariat to draft a Protocol on Employment and Labour that was adopted by the SADC Ministers and Social Partners for Employment and Labour meeting in Maputo, Mozambique, in May 2013. It has also contributed to the finalisation of the SADC Decent Work Programme, which will enable the member states to develop and implement common standards and priorities for improving work and living standards of workers and their families. Key areas of this document were approved at the Maputo meeting.

The Association of SADC Chambers of Commerce and Industry

The Association of SADC Chambers of Commerce and Industry (ASCCI) is a regional private-sector apex organisation that brings together SADC national chambers of commerce and industry, trade associations and employer organisations from all the member states. Mandated to be the voice of the private sector, ASCCI aims to enhance the private sector's role in the regional integration agenda. ASCCI has complained that SADC has sidelined the business community, including the private sector and informal businesses, in the regional economic integration process, as they have not been adequately consulted or incorporated in its efforts.

The SADC Council of Non-Governmental Organisations

The SADC Council of Non-Governmental Organisations (SADC-CNGO) was formed in 1998 by CSOs and the SADC Secretariat to facilitate meaningful engagement of the people of the region with the SADC Secretariat at the regional level, and with the member states at national level through national NGO umbrella bodies. It was created at a time when regional bodies such as the AfDB, the UN agencies and the World Bank were setting up their NGO committees. The formation of the SADC-CNGO created a common platform for CSOs to address issues of poverty alleviation, democratisation and good governance, ending internal political conflicts that have characterised the civil society landscape of SADC. Its membership is mainly national councils of NGOs in member states. It facilitates the engagement of civil society with member states, particularly on issues of the Regional Poverty Observatory and on political issues. The SADC-CNGO organises a civil society forum on the sidelines of official SADC meetings, generally in the country where the Summit is hosted. (The only exception was in 2011, when the meeting was held in South Africa after Angola placed restrictions on granting visas to civil society.) At these meetings, also attended by officials from the Secretariat and government ministers from member states, civil society hands over its communiqué to officials of the SADC Secretariat or the Chair.

According to the SADC-CNGO's Policy Paper on SADC Governance and Accountability:

- One of the biggest problems civil society is grappling with is the closed and state-centric nature of SADC. Agendas of ordinary Council of Ministers and Summit meetings are hidden from them and the peoples of the region. This is contrary to the practice at African Union level where Assembly agendas ... are posted on the African Union website. CSOs therefore find it difficult to engage with and input into SADC processes if crucial information is only the preserve of the Secretariat and government officials. It is even difficult to get an annual calendar of key, even statutory meetings, in order to inform planning and participation by non-state actors.

To enhance citizens' participation, SADC-CNGO has launched a SADC Protocols Tracker aimed at tracking and reporting on the level of signing, ratification and implementation of SADC protocols and other policy documents.

Following the decision by the SADC Summit to establish the SADC Regional Poverty Observatory in August 2008, a proposal on the technical and institutional frameworks of the Observatory was approved by the Council of Ministers and endorsed by the Summit in August 2010. The SADC-CNGO, in cooperation with the Southern Africa Trust, is partnering with SADC in the implementation of the Observatory by providing capacity. One of the outputs of the observatory will be a SADC Common Poverty Matrix.

The Regional Poverty Observatory

The SADC Secretariat has been collaborating with the Southern Africa Trust in implementing a decision by the SADC Summit of 2008 that aimed to set up a Regional Poverty Observatory by September 2013. Though it has been delayed, the Observatory will function as a forum where all stakeholders working in poverty eradication at the regional and national levels meet to evaluate and monitor the implementation of the Regional Poverty Reduction Framework. It is designed as a multi-stakeholder consultative forum for monitoring the objectives, targets and actions identified within the SADC poverty reduction programme.

The objectives of the Regional Poverty Observatory are to:

• Help member states through harmonisation of standards, methods and indicators;

• Speed up reforms and execution of national poverty reduction strategies;

• Provide regional best practices to supplement the benchmarks of the Millennium Development Goals; and

• Allow comparative performance analysis across member states.

Considering that poverty eradication is a priority focus of SADC, it is important to ensure adequate monitoring of poverty and progress toward the Millennium Development Goals.

The Southern Africa Trust has supported SADC in the design and the establishment of the Regional Poverty Observatory and is a member of the SADC Advisory Group. The Trust has also supported the establishment of national poverty observatories.

4.6.3 Other civil society initiatives

Southern African Peoples' Solidarity Network

The Southern African People's Solidarity Network (SAPSN) is a network supported by the Economic Justice Network of the Fellowship of Councils of Churches in Eastern and Southern Africa (FOCESSA). FOCESSA, SATUCC and the SADC-CNGO have an agreement recognising them as the apex bodies for civil society working at SADC level.

SAPSN brings together CSOs that are interested in SADC but do not fit under the SADC-CNGO or SATUCC umbrellas. These include rural activists, mining activists, women's movements and small-scale farmers from around the region. They organise a People's Summit in the wings of SADC Summit meetings under the banner "Reclaiming SADC for People's Solidarity and Development". They are mainly concerned with the deepening global crisis and increasing power of corporations over governments and community leaders.

The key areas discussed at People's Summits are:

• Food sovereignty;

• The extractive industry;

• Energy and megaprojects;

• Land and water grabs;

• Ecological justice; and

• Alternative regionalism.

The SAPSN aim is to create and strengthen the influence of people's movements in the region and to make governments and corporations accountable to the people, as well as to "point to alternatives to the 'opening up' and deepening exploitation of our peoples and countries within the neoliberal globalised capitalist economy".

The Southern Africa Gender Protocol Alliance

The Southern Africa Gender Protocol Alliance (SGPA) was established in 2005 and campaigned for the adoption – and now the implementation – of the SADC Protocol on Gender and Development. The SGPA consists of national networks of gender NGOs and country theme clusters. Currently, it comprises 15 country networks, nine theme groups and two interest groups.

The Protocol on Gender and Development was adopted by the SADC Heads of State and Government at the 2008 Summit as a global first, providing as it did a "road map to equality" by setting 28 realistic, measurable targets, time frames by 2015 and indicators for achieving gender equality in line with Millennium Development Goal 3. This provides a key mobilising tool for governments and civil society.

Since 2011, the SGPA has been working closely with the SADC Gender Unit to provide technical assistance to national gender machineries to update national gender policies and develop costed gender action plans that are aligned to the Protocol. Gender Links is working with partners including members of the SGPA and local governments to conduct village-level workshops to raise awareness on the key provisions of the Protocol among citizens. This is aimed at empowering citizens, especially women, to use the instrument to hold their respective governments to account and enhance their capacity to use the instrument to claim their rights. To enhance ownership, the SGPA country focal networks are identifying champions for each of the 28 targets at national level. Initiatives such as a Knowledge Quiz, Attitudes Quiz and Citizen Score Card are tools used to measure citizens' engagement with the Protocol.

The member states hold summits to review progress in the 28 areas of the Protocol and to reward institutions and individuals who contribute to that progress. A Barometer has been developed to monitor achievement of Protocol targets. The key feature of the Barometer is the Southern Africa Gender and Development Index introduced in 2011, based on empirical data on 23 indicators.

4.7 Current debates in SADC

4.7.1 The challenge of multiple REC memberships

Most members of SADC are also members of other regional bodies, including the RECs formally recognised by the AU, creating overlapping memberships that carries the risk of competing agendas. Countries tend to cherry-pick what they want from the different RECs. Table 4.11 lists cross-memberships in RECs by SADC member states.

Table 4.11 Cross-memberships in RECs by SADC member states

Member state	Other regional bodies the state belongs to
Angola	Economic Community of Central African States (ECCAS)
Botswana	Southern African Customs Union (SACU)
DRC	Common Market for Eastern and Southern Africa (COMESA)
Lesotho	SACU
Madagascar	COMESA, Indian Ocean Commission (IOC)
Malawi	COMESA
Mauritius	COMESA, IOC
Namibia	SACU
Seychelles	COMESA, IOC
South Africa	Brazil, Russia, India, China and South Africa (BRICS), SACU
Swaziland	COMESA, SACU
Tanzania	East African Community (EAC)
Zambia	COMESA
Zimbabwe	COMESA

Eight SADC member states – DRC, Malawi, Mauritius, Madagascar, Seychelles, Swaziland, Zambia and Zimbabwe – belong to COMESA, while Angola is a member of the Economic Community of Central African States (ECCAS) and Tanzania is in the East African Community (EAC). Botswana, Lesotho, Namibia, South Africa and Swaziland are members of the Southern African Customs Union (SACU). Only Mozambique has been "loyal" to SADC in that it does not belong to another REC (Figure 4.6).

SADC therefore faces a challenge of multiple memberships, with member states participating in other regional economic, political and security cooperation schemes that may compete with or undermine each other. In addition, the member states face challenges such as lack of financial and human capacity to deal with the similar obligations but different time frames and targets outlined by the different RECs, with a resultant challenge in the prioritisation of issues.

SADC is also joining with the Common Market for Eastern and Southern Africa (COMESA) and the EAC to form the African Free Trade Zone. The leaders of the three trading blocs have agreed to create a single free trade zone, consisting of 26 countries with a GDP of an estimated USD 624 billion. It is hoped the African Free Trade Zone Agreement will ease access to markets within the zone and end problems arising from the fact that several of the member countries belong to multiple groups. The Africa Free Trade Zone will create a Free Trade Area (FTA) spanning the whole continent from the Cape to Cairo. This is premised on a tripartite process that aims to remove barriers to trade amongst the members of COMESA, SADC and the EAC, to institute trade facilitation measures and to harmonise customs procedures. Ultimately, the tripartite process is aimed at providing a single option for rationalisation of the COMESA, SADC and EAC regional integration agendas, bringing closer the realisation of the AEC under the AU.

Figure 4.6 Regional integration initiatives in eastern and southern Africa

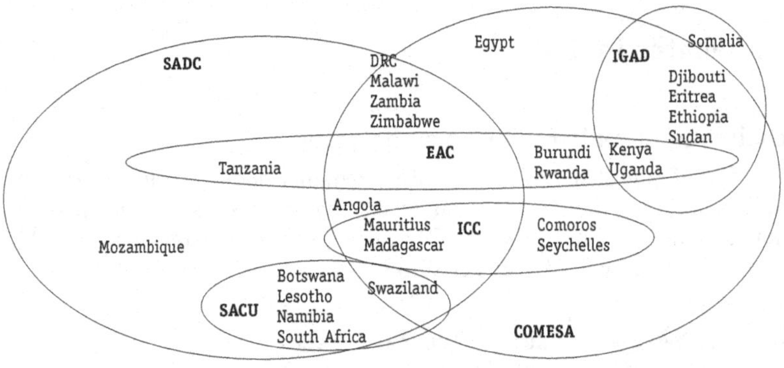

Source: Kalaba (2007) adapted from Olympio et al. (IGAD – Intergovernmental Authority on Development)

4.7.2 Negotiations with the EU on Economic Partnership Agreements

The following seven countries are negotiating an Economic Partnership Agreement (EPA) with the EU under the SADC grouping – Angola, Botswana, Lesotho, Mozambique, Namibia, Swaziland and South Africa. South Africa initially participated as an observer and in a supportive capacity until it formally joined negotiations in 2007. The remaining eight SADC countries – DRC, Madagascar, Malawi, Mauritius, Seychelles, Tanzania, Zambia and Zimbabwe – are negotiating as part of the East and Southern Africa grouping.

The SADC EPA negotiations are complicated by the pre-existing Trade, Development and Cooperation Agreement that South Africa has with the EU. Botswana, Lesotho, Mozambique, and Swaziland have signed interim EPAs with the EU, whereas South Africa, Namibia and Angola did not sign the interim EPAs, citing serious flaws in terms of the process, substance and timetable. They have called for open and frank discussions on all these issues. However, the fact that some countries have signed while others have not, signals the weakening of the regional approach to the negotiations, which resulted from the adoption of a two-step approach to the negotiations by the EU in late 2007. The signing of EPAs by individual countries contradicted the position and advice of the AU, which declared in 2009 that: "The [AU] and RECs ... coordinate EPA configurations in Africa with a view to harmonising the key issues of common interest to Africa in the EPA negotiations in order to enable Africa to speak with one voice."

4.7.3 The SADC Free Trade Area

The RISDP provides indicators to assess the progress of the harmonisation and convergence process among the member states of the SADC. It gives a road map and milestones to guide member states in achieving macro-economic convergence. Its targets included the attainment of an FTA by 2008, a Customs Union by 2010, a Common Market by 2012, a Monetary Union by 2016 and the elimination of exchange rate controls. Some of these targets are being reviewed as a result of the economic crisis taking place in the Eurozone.

The FTA was launched in September 2008. Out of the 15 member states, 12 are already participating in the FTA. Participating member states have embarked on elimination of tariffs and non-tariff barriers on substantially all trade. However, for SACU countries this process was completed in 2007; for Mozambique it will be complete in 2015 because of the tariff offer it has with South Africa. Zimbabwe had been granted derogation to suspend the tariff phase-down of category C products, which started in 2010–2012. Reductions will start in 2012–2014.

4.7.4 The Policy Dialogue Programme

In recognition of the importance of quality policy research and analysis in developing the SADC strategies, the Secretariat initiated the SADC Policy Analysis and Dialogue Programme in 2011 and budgeted for pilot implementation in 2012/2013. The purpose of this initiative is to enhance policy dialogue among key stakeholders at both member-state and regional levels, designed to feed into the deliberations and discussions in the SADC policy organs and other intergovernmental processes.

Bibliography and resources

Books and articles

Chimanikire, DP (2002) *Southern African Development Community: The Role of the Organ on Politics, Defence and Security (OPDS)*. Trade and Development Studies Centre Issue No. 20. Harare, Zimbabwe

DBSA (2012) *SADC Environmental Legislation Handbook*, 3rd edn

Hartzenberg, T, Ncube, P & Tekere, M (2002) *Trade Relations in the 21st Century: Focus on the Southern African Development Community*. Zimbabwe: SAPES

Jauch, H (2001) *Building a Regional Labour Movement: The Southern African Trade Union Coordinating Council SATUCC*. SATUCC, Labour Resource and Research Institute (LaRRI), Namibia

Khosa, M, Mupimbila, C & Ragasamy, L (1996) Models of economic integration. In J Whitman (ed.) *Pulling Together: The Sustainability Challenge for Southern Africa*. Global Security Fellows Initiative: University of Cambridge (Working Draft). pp. 27–28

Musavengana, T (2011) The proposed SADC Parliament: Old wine in new bottles or an idea whose time has come? *Institute of Security Studies*

SADC/GIZ (2013) *Strengthening SADC National–Regional Linkages: Final Report*. DPC and Associates

SADCC (1988) *SADCC: A Handbook*. Gaborone Printing and Publishing Company

SADC-CNGO (2011) *SADC Governance and Accountability: Perspectives from Civil Society*. SADC-CNGO Policy Paper Series, Regional Policy Paper 4

SADC-CNGO (2011) *SADC Governance and Accountability: Perspectives from Civil Society*. SADC-CNGO Policy Paper Series, Regional Policy Paper 4

Websites

www.sadcreview.com. Accessed on 2 January 2013.

www.sadc.int. Accessed on 3 January 2013.

www.au.int. Accessed on 3 January 2013.

Reports

African Capacity Building Foundation (2008) A Survey of The Capacity Needs of Africa's Regional Economic Communities. Colorado.

African Union Commission (2010) Minimum Integration Programme 2009–2012

Empowering women to claim their rights: Village level workshops on the SADC Protocol on Gender and Development Report. Gender Links

SADC, Report of the Executive Secretary (Activity Report of the SADC Secretariat) 2011–2012

SADC, The Regional Poverty Reduction Framework Regional Economic Integration: A Strategy for Poverty Eradication Towards Sustainable Development. 18–20 April 2008, Pailles, Mauritius

Schreiner, B, Mtsweni, A & Pegram, G, An Institutional Framework for Stakeholder Participation in Trans-Boundary Basins. Water Research Commission

Southern African Peoples' Solidarity Network (SAPSN) Facilitating Social Movements in SADC: Reclaiming SADC for People's Development – A People's SADC Myth or Reality?

SADC contacts

SADC Liaison Office at the AU

Head: Ms Nomatamsanqa Sopazi
+251 929 180058
nsopazi@sadc.int

AU Headquarters
Building C, Ground Floor, Roosevelt Street (Old Airport Area) / PO Box 3243
W12 K19, Addis Ababa, Ethiopia

AU Liaison Office at the SADC Secretariat

Head: Dr Al Hadji Sarjoh Bah
+267 758 26121
bahs@africa-union.org

SADC Secretariat
P/Bag 0095
Gaborone, Botswana

Organ on Politics, Defence and Security Affairs

Director: Jorge C. Cardoso
+267 3641601
jcardoso@sadc.int

SADC Secretariat
Plot 54385 CBD / Post Bag 0095
Gaborone, Botswana

Printed in the United States
By Bookmasters